Southwest Flavor

Adela Amador's TALES FROM THE KITCHEN

Recipes and stories from
New Mexico Magazine

Eufemia Amador, Adela's mother, in 1966 at age 68

NEW MEXICO
MAGAZINE

Adela Amador

Photo: Steve Larese

Author: Adela Amador

Editors: Emily Drabanski

          Walter K. Lopez

Book design and illustrations: Bette Brodsky

Publisher: Ethel Hess

Library of Congress Catalog Card Numbers:

00-130648

ISBN: 0-937206-61-X

Printed in Korea

Introduction 6

Fall
Page 65

Winter
Page 93

INTRODUCTION

I was born in La Madera in Río Arriba County in 1924. I am the fourth of 12 children, all of whom are still living. When my father was asked how many children he had, he said, "Twelve."

With surprise, they asked, "Are they all living?"

He answered, *"Unos vivos, y unos tontos; pero todos comen."* (Some are bright and some are dull, but they all eat!")

Shortly after I was born, the family moved to Ojo Caliente, where my father worked building cabins at the hot springs. He followed carpentry jobs, wherever they were. In 1930, we moved to Placitas at the foot of the Sandía Mountains. Between the grade school there and Our Lady of Sorrows in Bernalillo I finished the eighth grade. I went to Santa Cruz as a boarder at the Edith McCurdy School and graduated from there. I received a scholarship from Indiana Central College, but there was no way I could continue my education in the midst of the Great Depression. Instead I went to California and worked at Douglas Aircraft in order to help with the family income.

After the war, I married and had two children, Orlando and Armando, who have literally been the joy of my life. I remarried in 1970 and attended the University of New Mexico together with my boys. I received my degree in Spanish literature, with a minor in philosophy. During that stint, three of my *cuentos* were published in an anthology.

In 1980, I opened a drapery business, and have worked there since. I learned to cook from my mother, from county extension agents during the Depression, and later, from the home economics teacher at McCurdy School. She opened a whole new world to us and taught us how to use available ingredients and make them into palatable foods. I have been writing "Southwest Flavor" for *New Mexico Magazine* since January 1993 and have enjoyed wonderful contacts with my readers everywhere.

✜

New Mexico before World War II was very provincial. Life was simple and subsistence farming was the basis of life. New Mexico cuisine has come basically from the Native Americans, who first domesticated the essential plants. They ate simple combinations of chile, beans, corn, squash and meat. Years ago the meat was wild game, especially rabbit and deer. Chickens, sheep and cattle came from Europe later.

Even after the arrival of the Europeans, small, sparsely populated communities were isolated because of poor transportation. Foods remained as they had been for centuries. Even today in out-of-the-way communities old folks will tell you, "That's not the way to make *chiles rellenos*!" or "Beans should not be cooked in a pressure cooker!"

In our family foods were simple: the same corn, squash, beans and chile were basics. We ate green vegetables and fruits from the garden all summer, and canned or dried in the winter. Green chile and squash were dried and later reconstituted by adding water before cooking. Red chile was made into *ristras*, and when well dried, was ground into chile powder, as it is today. Apples and apricots were also dried and mostly eaten as snacks.

Bartering was a way of acquiring foods we did not raise. My father took apples in his pick-up truck and traded for pinto beans in the Estancia Valley, which was at one time the bean capital of dry farming and provided the best pinto beans ever. Potatoes were brought from southern Colorado. We traded apples for beans and potatoes, measure for measure. We traded with our San Felipe neighbors for corn for the animals and blue cornmeal that we used as cereal.

An Italian family who settled in our village introduced us to spaghetti sometime in the late '30s. Goat cheese was the only cheese available, from a neighbor who had a herd of goats. We ate it as a dessert, with either sugar or honey. I remember eating very little rice, and only in soups or as a dessert which we called *arroz dulce*. We never had what is now called Spanish rice.

We were lucky to have lived on a farm, where we raised animals that provided us with milk, eggs and meat. Rabbits and chickens supplied most of the meat. A pig or two, butchered in the fall, furnished meat and lard, which was very important for frying foods and making tortillas. We had no fear of cholesterol then.

Enchiladas, tacos, chimichangas, burritos, chalupas and tamales are all recent arrivals. All these dishes come from the same few kettles: green chile, red chile, beans whole or refried, corn or wheat flour tortillas, tomatoes, lettuce and cheese. These dishes are all served attractively, in different ways and given different names.

In our family we made – and still make – tortillas *gorditas*, thick, fat ones so they can be opened and filled, making a sandwich. They are made from wheat flour, not cornmeal. At one time they were used as spoons. Before there were spoons, there were tortillas. Foods were prepared in such a way that they could be scooped up with two pieces of tortilla.

The corn tortillas, which are the main staple in so many of those new dishes, are recent arrivals from Mexico – by way of California and Arizona – although we must give the Native Americans credit for first inventing them. It was they who boiled the corn to remove the hull and make a mash that was dried and made into dough for tortillas. Nowadays, they are factory-made, and inexpensive compared to the formidable task of trying to make them at home.

My mother did not often make tortillas, even though we children loved them. She made bread in the backyard *horno* almost every week and tortillas only in the interim. Tortillas were much more work and time-consuming, and used up more flour and lard. She had learned to make bread from her mother, my grandmother, who was so proud of her Spanish heritage that she thought tortillas were by Mexicans and for Mexicans. My grandmother often said so disparagingly. She also disliked the *horno* and always cooked her bread in the oven. My mother preferred the *horno* because she could bake many more loaves at one time. My sisters and I have all followed this family tradition of baking our own bread.

Caring for animals, planting, gathering and preserving food were all family affairs, and the children were never too small to help.

Then came the war, which scattered family members throughout the world. Young men were taken into military service, and whole families moved to areas where employment was available in war factories. I helped make C-47s in California. We found a big world out there, and saw things and learned to do things we had never seen or done before.

Traditional values were changing. There was no more bartering; we had entered the money economy. We were experiencing the light of a new day. Now it was money in exchange for our labor.

Traditional foods today have become almost an exception, even though they use the same ingredients. What we eat today is a woven blend of many cultures, prepared with pride. They are a symbol of the past and the present, and provide a link in the chain of our Southwest heritage.

People who come to New Mexico to study or to play enjoy the foods we have. Those who come to stay share with us their best, and change happens. The traditions we most cherish are easily lost, so we must keep them alive, or try to revive them for generations to come.

Spring

Spring sneaks in between cold and windy days. We never know the minute it arrives, or when it is here to stay. The light has returned, and the sky is a true blue. The Earth has awakened, and although we can't see it all, we feel it. White fluffy clouds appear in the sky and ripples of rain come as spring showers. Green fills the shadows and windy places. Early bulbs slowly poke out of the ground to offer an array of color in the garden. Early birds crowd the feeders and thank us with their lovely song.

TREATS FOR A WINDY DAY

The Ides of March is coming. In New Mexico, this usually is a cold, dry and windy month. The wind comes to annoy humans and destroy what isn't nailed or firmly anchored down. A person seems to need protection from the wind more than from cold or snow, so we retreat to the sanctuary of our car, office or home as fast as we can run.

We think of all the bad things the wind does, such as blowing roofs off porches, breaking tree branches and strewing them all over the streets, messing up traffic lights and threatening to blow us off the freeway, if we are driving small cars. But we must not forget that wind is also a powerful force for good.

Perhaps the wind was once used to turn the millstone that ground the grain. Grinding was a tedious job that was done daily with hand tools, such as *metates*. Later the wind was used to pump water. The Plains People must have been delighted with the windmill, when they no longer had to haul water for cattle, or to rely on nearby watering holes.

I remember my father getting rotors from Montgomery Ward and unpacking them on the kitchen floor, while reading directions on how to assemble them. He put rotors together in the yard and then built a tower. It took many days. When he was finished, the wind pumped the water from the well into a small tank for home use and into a bigger tank for sheep and irrigation. Later, he installed many windmills for other people.

Children are more interested in what gives them pleasure. The wind reminds them of kites. The first time my boys came home from school all excited about kites, I was completely unprepared. As a child I never played with a kite and certainly never made one. With children, everything must happen this minute. They can't wait! It was either make a kite or drive 14 miles to the nearest store and buy one. No way!

They had ideas and we found materials at hand. I suggested a fish kite – don't ask me why! We traced and cut two large fish out of brown wrapping paper about 24 inches long and maybe 12 inches wide, and sewed them together, except for the big mouth. Two strips of balsa wood were sewed in place to make the crosspiece, old hosiery made up the tail and a ball of string attached it to a boy. It worked! They had a lot of fun capturing the wind, running up and down the fields. I was surprised that it worked at all. Sometimes we are blessed in our ignorance.

Running in the wind made two young boys very hungry. Tamale pie was always a favorite of theirs.

Tamale Pie

1 medium onion, chopped

1 teaspoon fat

2 cups lean chopped or ground beef

2 cups fresh or canned tomatoes, cut fine

2 pimientos, chopped fine

2 tablespoons red chile powder

1 clove garlic, chopped fine

1 teaspoon salt

*Cornmeal mush

Fry onion in fat in pan until light brown.

❖ Add meat and fry five minutes or until red disappears.

❖ Add tomatoes, pimientos, chile powder, garlic and salt; stir well.

❖ Line a large greased pie pan with a layer of cornmeal mush; place meat mixture in pan and spread to edge.

❖ Cover meat mixture with broken pats of mush, leaving spaces for color to show through.

❖ Bake at 350 degrees for one hour and 30 minutes.

❖ Baking time may be shortened by cooking meat longer.

❖ Vary the recipe by adding a cup of cooked pinto beans, or simplify using prepared chile as a filling.

*Cornmeal mush: See opposite page.

Cornmeal Mush

3 cups boiling water

1 cup yellow or white cornmeal

1 teaspoon salt

1 cup cold water

* Heat to boiling three cups water in saucepan.
* Mix cornmeal and salt with one cup cold water.
* Pour into boiling water, stirring constantly.
* Cook until thickened, stirring constantly.
* Cover and continue cooking over low heat for 10 minutes or longer.
* Yield: 6 servings.

Pineapple Upside-Down Pie

Now let's try an upside-down pie instead of the upside-down cake that we're so familiar with. This nut-topped pie makes its own luscious caramel sauce as it bakes.

Pastry for 2-crust pie
1 can (1 pound 4 1/2 ounces) pineapple tidbits (reserve syrup)
water
3 tablespoons cornstarch
3/4 cup brown sugar, firmly packed
2 tablespoons lemon juice
6 tablespoons butter
1/2 cup pecan halves

❖ Drain pineapple. Add water to pineapple syrup to make 1 1/4 cups.

❖ Combine cornstarch and 1/4 cup brown sugar in saucepan.

❖ Add lemon juice and pineapple syrup mixture; cook, stirring constantly, until mixture is thick and clear.

❖ Remove from heat and add 2 tablespoons butter, stirring until it melts.

❖ Add pineapple.

❖ While preheating oven, place remaining 4 tablespoons butter in bottom of 9-inch pie pan.

❖ Sprinkle with remaining 1/2 cup brown sugar and 1 tablespoon water.

❖ Arrange pecan halves, rounded side down, around bottom and sides of pan.

❖ Carefully line pan with pastry. Spoon in pineapple mixture.

❖ Adjust top crust, flute edges, cut vents.

❖ Place pie on square of foil in oven to catch drippings.

❖ Bake in hot oven (425 degrees) 25 minutes.

❖ Turn out, upside down, on serving plate immediately.

❖ Cool on rack before cutting.

❖ Serve with ice cream or whipped cream, if desired.

Breakfast Casserole

8 slices bread

1 pound sausage

1 pound cheese

8 eggs

3/4 teaspoon salt

3/4 teaspoon dry mustard

Dash cayenne pepper

3 cups milk

6 large fresh mushrooms, cut up

2 bunches green onions, cut up

❖ Place slices of bread at bottom of 13-inch by 9-inch by 2-inch pan. Fry the sausage and remove from skillet into another dish.

❖ Grate cheese.

❖ In a large bowl beat together milk, eggs, salt, mustard and pepper.

❖ Place a layer of sausage, mushrooms and green onions over bread slices. Cover with grated cheese. Make another layer with remaining ingredients and top with cheese.

❖ Pour milk and egg mixture on top.

❖ Refrigerate covered overnight.

❖ Cover and cook at 350 degrees for one hour. Remove cover for last 10 minutes to let it brown.

Green Chile Stew

2 pounds pork cut in chunks

2 fresh tomatoes, or 1 pint of canned tomatoes

2 cups cubed potatoes

1 large chopped onion

2 cloves garlic, minced

2 cups chopped green chile

❖ Boil meat until done, then add the remaining ingredients.

❖ Simmer for another 1/2 hour, or until potatoes are done.

Flour Tortillas

4 cups flour
2 teaspoons baking powder
4 tablespoons shortening
1 1/2 teaspoons salt
1 1/2 cups warm water

❖ Sift flour, baking powder and salt together.
❖ Add shortening and water.
❖ Knead dough until well mixed and form into balls about 3 inches in diameter.
❖ Roll out into round flat-shaped cakes about 1/8-inch thick and cook on griddle separately until both sides are spotted medium brown.
❖ Cook both sides.
❖ Makes about 1 dozen.

LENTEN FOODS

I n small towns in northern New Mexico, this time of year is celebrated in prayer and meditation, and also with gusto.

On Wednesday, Thursday and Friday of Holy Week, the villagers have what they call *el encuentro* (the meeting). The priest comes down the lane to meet the congregation, which has gathered to walk toward the church. He leads them up the hill and into the church where he says Mass. He then leads them to the community house, where they feast together.

Later, they go back into the church, where the Stations of the Cross are observed. This is repeated all three days. The people find a community spirit in the traditions.

Sometimes this spirit has been disrupted, either by excommunication (which happened in villages years ago), or because the population has moved away and the priest no longer goes there, or because people have gone to other communities. For various reasons these traditions have almost disappeared.

The sharing of foods was part of the custom. Children were sent to the neighbors during the week, to inquire what each one was cooking or baking, so each family would have something different to share. It kept the women from working so hard, and still provided variety for the gatherings. The food almost always included fresh bread, *sopa* (bread pudding), *torta de huevo* and various foods made out of corn and rice.

Here are two Lenten foods prepared and eaten especially during Holy Week:

Torta de Huevo

15 to 18 red chile pods

3 cups water

2 tablespoons flour

2 tablespoons cooking oil

2 cloves garlic, crushed

Salt

3 eggs

1 tablespoon cracker crumbs

❖ Remove the stems and seeds from the chile pods, wash and dry.

❖ Place the chile on a cookie sheet and bake at 350 degrees until pods are soft.

❖ Puree pods and water to a paste in blender.

❖ Mix flour and oil and brown.

❖ Add chile puree, bring to a boil and simmer to the consistency of gravy.

❖ Add crushed garlic and salt to taste.

❖ Simmer an additional 30 minutes.

❖ Separate eggs.

❖ Beat egg yolks and add cracker crumbs.

❖ Beat egg whites until stiff, and fold in egg yolks.

❖ Drop mixture by tablespoons into hot oil and brown on both sides.

❖ Drain on paper towels, and add them to the red chile.

This dish was popular because red chile was always available, dried in *ristras* from the previous year's crop, and the chickens were laying eggs in plentiful numbers in the spring. Eggs were used in place of meat during Lent because on certain days the church prohibited eating meat. *Torta de Huevo* is excellent served with beans and tortillas.

Sopa

(also called *capirotada*)

14 slices of bread (any kind)

2 cups sugar

3 1/2 cups water

1 teaspoon cinnamon

5 tablespoons butter

1 cup raisins

1/2 cup piñon or pecan nuts

1 1/2 teaspoons vanilla

1 cup shredded cheese (Jack or Longhorn)

1 cup whipped cream, for garnish

1/2 cup sweet wine (optional)

❖ Butter ovenproof baking dish.

❖ Tear bread into 1-inch pieces and toast in 350-degree oven for 10 minutes.

❖ Toss bread and nuts in mixing bowl.

❖ Place sugar in saucepan over medium heat and stir continuously until sugar melts and turns caramel color.

❖ Add water immediately, being very careful because the syrup will bubble and splatter. Caramel might partially solidify but will liquefy as it reheats.

❖ Reduce heat and add raisins, vanilla and butter to caramel syrup while still hot.

❖ Stir until butter melts and pour syrup mixture over bread mixture. If not entirely soaked, add sweet wine as needed.

❖ Place mixture in baking dish and top with cheese.

❖ Bake at 350 degrees for 30 minutes.

❖ Serve with whipped cream or ice cream.

There were no supermarkets when I was a child, and the nearest grocery store was seven miles away over a dirt road. We didn't have candy bars or chocolate cake, but we did manage to have some sweets, mostly made with what was available and inexpensive. *Sopa* used up stale bread, if any was around, and with some sugar and a few spices made a great dessert. Of course, the formula changes, and there are many variations of this dish.

As children we certainly didn't know anything about the Easter Bunny, or baskets full of jellybeans and such things. Perhaps being isolated helped. We were taught that the Lord had risen and we accepted that with the coming of spring. Easter Sunday was a day for eating what had not been around during Lent, namely, meat. Also, we colored eggs, using food coloring, paper, crayons and paste. We had our ways of having fun.

Another part of Easter was that my sisters and I each received a new frock, made by our mother out of colorful gingham bought from the mercantile company. Since there were several dresses to make, she would buy a bolt of fabric, and we all had dresses of the same color, usually made from the same pattern. One Easter Sunday, we were allowed to wear our new dresses to go to the hillside and hide our colored eggs. Before we were ready to go home, it started to rain – one of those hard spring showers. We ran home as fast as we could, but not before the rain drenched us and left our little dresses with almost no color in them at all. Dyes were not colorfast in those days. Our mother usually did the first washing in salt water to try and hold the dye. But not this time. The first washing was that rainstorm, and red and green dyes were running down our legs, coloring our socks and shoes. We ended up with almost-white Easter dresses.

New Mexico Quiche

Crust:

1 cup flour

1/2 teaspoon salt

1/3 cup plus 1 tablespoon shortening

1 tablespoon red chile powder

Filling:

3/4 cup grated cheddar cheese

1/2 cup grated Monterey Jack cheese

3 large eggs, lightly beaten

1 teaspoon salt

1 1/2 cups Half-and-Half

1 cup chopped green chile

1/2 cup bacon bits

1/4 cup finely chopped green onions

❖ Preheat oven to 350 degrees.

❖ Mix flour, salt, shortening and chile powder.

❖ Mix with fork until dough holds together. Form into a smooth ball and roll out to fit 9-inch pan.

❖ Mix cheeses together and spread on bottom of pastry shell.

❖ Beat eggs in medium-size bowl; add remaining ingredients and pour over cheese-covered pastry.

❖ Bake 40-45 minutes or until knife inserted comes out clean.

Lite Bran Muffins

2 tablespoons shortening

1/4 cup sugar

1 egg, well-beaten

3/4 cup milk

1 cup bran

1 cup flour

2 1/4 teaspoons baking powder

1/2 teaspoon salt

❖ Work shortening with spoon until creamy and fluffy.

❖ Add sugar gradually and continue to work with spoon until light.

❖ Add egg and milk and beat well. Add bran and mix well; allow to stand 20 minutes to soak up moisture.

❖ Sift together flour, baking powder and salt and add to bran mixture.

❖ Fill oiled muffin pans 2/3 full and bake at 400 degrees for 30 minutes.

Cheese Tortilla Torta

2 cups cooked turkey or chicken, cubed

1 (11 ounce) can Mexican-style corn, drained

2 cups or 2 (4 ounces) cans diced or chopped green chile, undrained

1/2 cup chopped red onion

1 (1 pound) container sour cream mixed with 1 tablespoon flour

2 (10 ounce) cans enchilada sauce or same amount of homemade chile sauce

12 corn tortillas, halved

10 ounces sharp cheddar cheese, shredded or 2 1/2 cups of your choice of cheese

1/4 cup sliced, pitted ripe black olives, if desired

❖ Preheat oven to 350 degrees.

❖ Lightly grease 13-inch by 9-inch by 2-inch baking dish.

❖ In medium bowl, combine turkey or chicken, corn, chile, red onion and half of the sour cream mixture.

❖ Pour enchilada sauce into another medium bowl.

❖ Dip 8 tortilla halves, one at a time, in sauce, arrange on bottom of prepared dish.

❖ Add half the meat mixture, spreading evenly with spatula to cover.

❖ Sprinkle 1 cup of cheese over meat layer. Add another layer of 8 dipped tortilla halves, the remaining meat mixture spread evenly, and 1 cup of cheese.

❖ Top with remaining 8 tortilla halves, dipped in sauce. Pour any remaining sauce over dish.

❖ Spoon remaining sour cream mixture into plastic food storage bag; snip off one corner. With this you can make a lattice design over top of dish, decorating here and there with green chile, or may be a design of your own.

❖ Sprinkle with cheese and bake 30 minutes or until bubbling.

❖ Let stand 15 minutes before serving.

Herb Bread

1/2 cup onions, chopped

3 tablespoons butter or margarine

1 cup, plus 2 tablespoons warm milk

1 tablespoon sugar

1 1/2 teaspoon salt

1/2 teaspoon dill seed

1/2 teaspoon dried basil

1/2 teaspoon dried rosemary, crushed

1 package (1/4 ounces) active dry yeast

3 to 3 1/2 cups all-purpose flour

❖ Melt butter or margarine in a skillet over low heat, sauté onion in butter until tender, about 8 minutes. Cool for 10 minutes.

❖ Place in a mixing bowl.

❖ Add milk, sugar, salt, herbs, yeast and three cups flour; beat until smooth. Add enough remaining flour to form a soft dough.

❖ Turn onto a floured board; knead until smooth and elastic, about 6-8 minutes.

❖ Place in a greased bowl, turning once to grease top.

❖ Cover and let rise in a warm place until doubled, about 45 minutes. Punch the dough down.

❖ Shape into a ball and place on a greased baking sheet. Cover and let rise again until doubled, about 45 minutes.

❖ Bake at 375 degrees for 25-30 minutes.

❖ Remove to a wire rack, brush with melted butter. Cool.

❖ Yield: 1 loaf.

THE STAPLES OF LIFE

T hrough the ages, civilizations have flourished with some of the most basic foods, such as potatoes, beans and rice. These foods were nourishing, but maybe not so tasty at times. Today, we are able to embellish these basic foods with spices, vegetables, sauces and dozens of combinations, which people in other places and earlier times were not able to do.

It isn't any wonder that potatoes are just about everyone's favorite food, a versatile staple from which cooks have created a host of recipes from plain to fancy, from simple side dishes to fries, from elegant hors d'oeuvres to soups and salads. The potato came from Peru, but makes us think of Ireland and how the survival or death of thousands of people depended on the potato.

When we think of beans in this part of the country we think of pinto beans, forgetting that there are many other kinds popular in other parts of the world. A friend from the Bahamas, who taught at the same school with my husband, once treated us to a traditional meal of beans and rice. The mixture contained black and red beans, peas, rice and more. As the food was boiling on the stove there was a kind of scum floating on the surface of the water. I asked what it was when I saw him skimming it off and washing the spoon under the kitchen faucet. He explained it was only the larvae of the weevil, which attacks the plant and bores a tiny hole in the bean or pea, and is only forced out by the boiling water. He laughed and said, "You wouldn't object to a wee bit of protein, would you?"

The province of Asturias in Spain is known for its beans, which they call *favas*. We had been there several weeks and were starved for a bowl of beans. Our landlady told us she was serving beans for supper, so we were delighted. When the *favada* came into view that evening, I was disappointed. They looked like lima beans, not our pinto beans. Nevertheless the smell was right, and even though the *señora* warned me that it was a very strong meal (*¡muy fuerte!*), I ate them *con gusto*, not one serving but three! They were delicious, and I learned that even though there is something distinctively different about each kind, there is also a familiar taste in all beans.

Rice has been the staple food of southern and eastern Asia for thousands of years. It is also a basic food in Spain. Spain exports rice to Japan. Spanish rice and *arroz con pollo* (rice with chicken) are well known here, brought by the Spaniards. In Spain the famous dish is called *paella*. I had never seen or tasted it until my visit to Spain 20 years ago. I found my first *paella* in Barcelona. We had met a couple of university students from New York. Together we found a restaurant advertising *paella* Valenciana, even though we were a long way from Valencia. For a small price, we were served a huge platter of brilliantly yellow rice, laced with all kinds of ingredients, many not known to us for sure. It was the best rice I had ever eaten.

The distinctive yellow color is from saffron, which has become ridiculously expensive. Well, not ridiculous when you remember what it is – the pistil of a rare flower. Several strands of it in a jar is a labor-intensive product. Here we can get what is called Mexican saffron for much less. Check the Mexican herb rack in the market. This is the petal of a different flower, and is used by the tablespoon, not the strand. It colors the rice orange, instead of yellow, but creates a very similar taste. My recipe uses Mexican saffron.

Paella

3- to 3-1/2-pound chicken fryer, cut up

2- to 3-pound pork roast, cut up

1/2 cup olive oil

1 large onion

6 medium tomatoes

2 bell peppers

2 tablespoons Mexican saffron

3 cups uncooked regular rice

4 cups chicken broth

4 cups water

3 tablespoons paprika

2 1/2 tablespoons salt

1 1/2 teaspoons pepper

1/2 teaspoon cayenne red pepper

1 10-ounce package frozen green peas

1 15-ounce can artichoke hearts, drained

1 8-ounce jar sliced pimientos, drained

1 12-ounce package quick frozen shrimp (optional)

1 pound any whitefish, cut into small pieces (optional)

❖ In heavy kettle or Dutch oven brown chicken and pork in olive oil. Remove from kettle and set aside. Add onion, tomatoes and bell peppers, and cook until onion is tender.

❖ Take a cup or so of broth and in it boil the Mexican saffron to release its goodness and color. Place this and the rest of the liquid in the kettle, stir in rice, add the spices, chicken and pork, cover tightly and simmer for 25 minutes.

❖ Stir in peas. If you wish to add shrimp or fish, stir that in at this point. Cover and simmer 15 minutes longer. Then carefully stir in artichoke hearts.

❖ Serve on a large platter and garnish with parsley and pimientos, arranging them artistically on the surface.

❖ The recipe serves about 15 people, and leftovers freeze well for use later.

When we told my uncle, Sabino Ulibarrí, that we would be serving *paella,* he replied, "I hope it's *pa' mi, también."* (*Pa'ella = para ella* = "for her." *Pa' mi = para mi* = "for me, also.")

Rice Pudding

Rice can be prepared with more variations than any other staple. There are not only main and side dishes, but also some of the best desserts. In my childhood, *arroz dulce* (sweet rice) was much more common than any cake or pie or cookie. Here is the best rice pudding recipe I have ever tried.

1 quart milk
1/2 cup rice
1/2 cup seedless raisins
1/2 cup granulated sugar
4 eggs
1 teaspoon vanilla
1/2 teaspoon salt
2 teaspoons lemon juice
1/2 teaspoon cream of tartar
1/2 cup sifted confectioners' sugar

❖ Combine milk, rice and raisins in 2-quart sauce pan. Cover and cook over low heat until rice is tender, about 45 minutes. Stir occasionally.

❖ When rice is done, preheat oven to 375 degrees.

❖ Grease a 1 1/2 quart casserole dish.

❖ Beat egg whites until foamy, stir in salt, cream of tartar and confectioners' sugar until stiff. Spoon this meringue over the top of rice pudding.

❖ Bake 20 minutes and serve either warm or cold. Makes about 6 servings.

Fajitas

4 cloves garlic, minced

1/4 cup lime juice

1/4 cup pineapple juice

4 tablespoons mescal or tequila

1/4 cup olive oil

salt, season to taste

2 pounds *fajitas* (strips of) chicken, pork or beef

6 green New Mexico chiles, roasted, peeled and seeded

2 large onions, sliced

❖ Blend together the garlic, lime juice, pineapple juice and strain the mixture into a bowl.

❖ Add the mescal or tequila, olive oil and salt.

❖ Add the *fajitas* and marinate 1 1/2 to 2 hours.

❖ Then broil, or fry, to your satisfaction and serve.

If you love onions, then you want what we call *encebollada*. To do this, cook your sliced onions in 3 tablespoons of olive oil with garlic until onions are well browned.

❖ Cut the chile into strips as you would the *fajitas* and add them to the marinated mixture.

❖ Place the mixture in a hot flour tortilla and fold it into a taco.

❖ This you can top with guacamole sauce, or you can leave the onions out, if you so wish.

Moist Rhubarb Coffee Cake

2 cups cake flour

1 teaspoon baking powder

1 teaspoon baking soda

1/2 teaspoon salt

1 cup firmly packed light brown sugar, plus 2 tablespoons

1 egg

1 cup plain low fat yogurt

1/2 cup applesauce

1 teaspoon vanilla

3 cups rhubarb, coarsely chopped

❖ Sift together cake flour, baking powder, baking soda and salt into a large bowl.

❖ Stir the cup of brown sugar and egg in the bowl.

❖ Stir in yogurt, applesauce and vanilla.

❖ Stir into flour mixture, until ingredients are almost blended.

❖ Quickly stir in diced, uncooked rhubarb until evenly mixed.

❖ Turn into 9-inch-square pan sprayed with non-stick vegetable spray.

❖ Sprinkle top evenly with remaining 2 tablespoons sugar.

❖ Bake at 350 degrees for 30 to 35 minutes or until cake tests done in center.

Chicken Cashew Casserole

1 (3 ounces) can chow mein noodles
1 can cream of chicken soup, undiluted
1/2 cup chicken broth
2 cups cooked chicken or turkey, diced
1 cup diced celery
1/4 cup minced onion
1/3 cup cashew nuts

❖ Set aside 1/2 cup of noodles.
❖ Combine all other ingredients and pour into 1 quart casserole dish.
❖ Sprinkle the half-cup of noodles over surface and bake for 35 minutes at 350 degrees.

Natillas

Milk Custard

1 pint milk
1/4 teaspoon salt
2 tablespoons flour
1 teaspoon vanilla
2 eggs
1/2 cup sugar

- Beat yolks and add to sugar, flour and salt.
- Add to hot milk and boil until it thickens.
- Add vanilla.
- Beat egg whites until stiff and fold into the *natillas*.
- This serves 4.
- Sprinkle with cinnamon.

Creamy Asparagus Casserole

2 pounds fresh asparagus, cut into 1-inch pieces

1/4 cup butter or margarine

1/4 cup flour

2 cups milk, or Half-and-Half cream

1/2 teaspoon salt

1/4 teaspoon pepper

6 hard-cooked eggs, sliced

1 cup shredded cheddar cheese

1 cup crushed potato chips

❖ Place asparagus in large saucepan with enough water to cover; cook until crisp-tender. Drain well and set aside.

❖ In a saucepan over medium heat, melt butter. Stir in flour until smooth.

❖ Gradually add milk. Bring to a boil over medium heat; cool and stir for 2 minutes.

❖ Add salt and pepper.

❖ Layer half the asparagus in an ungreased 11-inch by 7-inch by 2-inch baking dish.

❖ Cover with half the eggs, cheese and sauce. Repeat layers.

❖ Sprinkle with potato chips.

❖ Bake, uncovered, at 350 degrees for 30 minutes, or until heated through.

Rhubarb Custard Bars

2 cups flour

1/4 cup sugar

1 cup cold butter or margarine

Filling:

2 cups sugar

7 tablespoons flour

1 cup whipping cream

3 eggs, beaten

5 cups fresh rhubarb, finely chopped

Topping:

2 packages (3 ounces each) cream cheese, softened

1/2 cup sugar

1/4 teaspoon vanilla

1 cup whipping cream

❖ In a bowl, combine the flour and sugar, cut in butter until the mixture resembles coarse crumbs.

❖ Press into greased 13-inch by 9-inch by 2-inch baking pan.

❖ Bake at 350 degrees for 10 minutes.

❖ For filling: Combine sugar and flour in bowl. Whisk in cream and eggs. Stir in rhubarb. Pour over crust.

❖ Bake at 350 degrees for 40-45 minutes or until custard is set.

❖ Cool.

❖ For topping: Beat cream cheese, sugar and vanilla until smooth, fold in whipped cream. Spread over top. Cover and chill. Cut into bars.

❖ Yield: 3 dozen.

Summer

Summer days grow warm and soft. Everywhere there is love and songs, and nests and eggs. All living creatures seem to know that life is lovely, but brief. Trees and gardens are in full bloom, and the bees seek out the nectar. Other insects scurry around as if their life depended on speed, and it does. Hurry, for the days will soon grow shorter.

Here in the desert, we long for moisture. We get about half of our year's supply during this season. The amount is so little, "monsoon" isn't quite the right word, but we are grateful.

ADD SPICE TO YOUR LIFE

"May the wind under your wings carry you to where the sun sails and the moon walks."
—J.R.R. Tolkein

I think of June as my month, for it contains my birthday. When we were little girls, each sibling looked forward to that special day. We did not receive material gifts but the honored person was permitted to sleep later than usual, and also was excused from doing dishes. It was equivalent to Queen For a Day. What more could we ask for? When we grew up and had families of our own, we began the practice of giving birthday gifts and enjoy it to this day.

A few years ago, however, I had come to a crucial time in my life, and no longer wanted my birthday celebrated in the usual way. I guess I needed to prove to myself that I still had wings and could fly!

I convinced a friend and co-worker to go with me to Mesa Verde ruins near the New Mexico-Colorado border. I had been there before, but she had not. Never before in my life had I needed to check the car, tires, gas, room reservations or anything else involved in planning a trip. A man in my life had always been there for me. I had followed the leader and now I must follow, not only my own nose, but the signs on the road.

An artist friend of mine, Mike, made us a lovely sign that read, "Thelma and Louise." We placed it on the rear window of the car and took pictures with us on each side of it. Of course, we didn't drive away without removing the sign, for I think that would have been asking for trouble.

Our first stop was in Aztec, where we went into the Great Kiva. We were the only ones there, and so we sat quietly, listening to the drums and meditating. Next we went to see the long wall for which the ruins are famous, and walked all through the grounds. A multitude of tourists descended just as we were leaving.

We arrived in Durango, Colo., early enough to get a feel of the town, find our motel and look for a good restaurant. We celebrated with a margarita and an excellent meal. We watched some crazy movie on television and settled for the night.

I had totally forgotten how far the Mesa Verde ruins were from Durango and was glad we had started up the hill early. The cars were bumper-to-bumper and the parking was non-existent. We had to wait until someone moved out and then made a dash for the space. Our first glimpse of the masonry walls, half hidden behind piñon trees and hugging the sandstone cliffs, was enough to excite the dead. My friend's joy at seeing the ruins of this ancient civilization made her eyes shine. She stopped at every viewing sight, and walked through all the areas permitted. She climbed down and up the canyon many times in order not to miss a thing. Her enthusiasm made me believe the trip was worthwhile.

We rested another night and started back after breakfast. We had intended to get home early, but since we had not encountered any problems, I thought it would be a good idea to press our luck and take the road to Chaco Canyon. The dirt road was narrow and dusty and after some miles, I wondered if this had been a smart move. The day was very hot and dry and we only stopped at a few places, but instead of going back to the road we knew, we kept on going south and ended in Thoreau. We thought of all the "what ifs" because the road was almost washed out. Ruts were so deep the car hit bottom. My friend had the gall to ask about how much gas we had left. I looked at the gas gauge for the first time and realized we were almost empty. Yes, there were some anxious moments, for we never met another car on that road. They knew better!

It is strange how we live our lives under the assumption that we will live forever as a couple, seldom realizing that one day there will be only one of us. One will have to learn to function without the other. It is a good idea sometimes to fly alone. Each one could try doing alone what we usually do together. Visit a friend, hike alone, eat at a restaurant by yourself, and get a feel for such aloneness. It might not be pleasant but perhaps invaluable at some time in our lives.

The trip made it possible for me to map out my life differently and a wee bit more independently. My husband and I still live out our lives by twos, but my feeling is that now I would not crumble if I needed to face life alone. I needed to try my wings and found that they had grown since last clipped.

In June we have fresh greens and fruits from the garden for salads. I want to share with you some recipes for flavored vinegars that I have received from one of the home economists at the County Extension Service in Albuquerque.

Lemon Thyme Vinegar

❖ Remove peel (colored portion only) from 1 lemon in a thin spiral and place in a sterilized pint jar with 4 to 5 thyme sprigs.

❖ Heat distilled white vinegar to just below the boiling point.

❖ Fill jar with vinegar and cap tightly.

❖ Allow to stand 3 to 4 weeks.

❖ Strain vinegar into a clean sterilized jar, adding a new sprig of fresh thyme if desired.

❖ Seal tightly.

❖ Use in dressings for tossed green salads or marinades for vegetables.

Basil Garlic Vinegar

❖ Place 1/2 cup coarsely chopped fresh basil leaves and 2 cloves split peeled garlic in sterilized pint jar.

❖ Heat distilled white or wine vinegar to just below boiling point.

❖ Fill jar with vinegar and cap tightly.

❖ Allow to stand 3 to 4 weeks.

❖ Strain vinegar, discarding basil and garlic.

❖ Pour vinegar into a clean sterilized jar, adding a new sprig of fresh basil if desired. Seal tightly.

❖ Use in dressings for rice, pasta, antipasto salads or in flavored mayonnaise.

Raspberry Vinegar

❖ Bruise 1 cup fresh raspberries lightly and place in sterilized pint jar.

❖ Heat distilled white or wine vinegar to just below the boiling point.

❖ Fill jar with vinegar and cap tightly.

❖ Allow to stand 2 to 3 weeks.

❖ Strain vinegar, discarding fruit. Pour vinegar into a clean sterilized jar.

❖ Seal tightly.

❖ Use in dressings for mixed green or fruit salads, or in marinades for chicken.

❖

Asparagus, Chicken Apple Salad

1 cup cut fresh asparagus pieces

2 tablespoons cider vinegar

2 tablespoons vegetable oil

2 teaspoons honey

2 teaspoons minced fresh parsley

1/2 teaspoon salt

1/4 teaspoon pepper

1 cup cubed, cooked chicken

1/2 cup diced apples

2 cups torn mixed greens

❖ Cook asparagus in a small amount of water until crisp-tender, about 3-4 minutes, drain and cool.

❖ In a bowl, combine the next six ingredients. Stir in the chicken, apple and asparagus.

❖ Toss.

❖ Serve over greens.

❖ Garnish with alfalfa sprouts, if desired. Yield: 3 servings.

Nut Burgers

1/2 pound cashews, ground in a blender

1/2 pound walnuts, ground in a blender

1 cup cooked brown rice

1 cup grated Colby cheese, or any mild cheese

1 egg

1/2 onion, chopped

1 teaspoon sea salt

Chile powder for seasoning

Whole wheat flour or bread crumbs

Unrefined safflower oil for frying

❖ Mix first seven ingredients together and season to taste with chile powder, hot sauce or other seasoning.

❖ Shape into patties. When forming patties, dip hands in cold water before shaping each one, to prevent sticking to your hands.

❖ Roll in whole wheat flour or crumbs.

❖ Chill.

❖ Fry in hot oil.

❖

Broccoli & Cauliflower Salad

1 1/2 cups broccoli florets

1 1/2 cups cauliflower florets

1 (8 ounce) can water chestnuts, diced

Dressing:

1/2 cup mayonnaise

1/4 teaspoon salt

2 tablespoons lemon juice

1 tablespoon sugar

❖ Pour dressing over vegetables and toss gently.

Fruit Salad

1 can (11 ounces) mandarin oranges, drained

1 cup flaked coconut, toasted

1 cup miniature marshmallows

1 can (8 ounces) pineapple tidbits, drained

1 cup (8 ounces) sour cream

1/4 cup walnuts, chopped

2 tablespoons brown sugar

❖ In a bowl, combine the first five ingredients; mix well.

❖ Cover and refrigerate overnight.

❖ Just before serving, sprinkle with walnuts and brown sugar.

❖ Garnish with fresh mint, if desired.

IT'S RAINING
SNAKES & TOADS

"*Llueve sapos y culebras.*"

In English we say it's raining cats and dogs, or even pitchforks and hammer handles, but in Spanish our proverb says, "It's raining toads and snakes."

A tourist asked a New Mexico old-timer, "How much rain do you get here in the desert?" The old man answered, "About seven inches a year." Then he scratched his chin and stared off at the distant mountains and said, "Yeah, and I remember last year – I remember the afternoon it came."

July brings us those hot days, cool nights, and every now and then, rain by the bucketful. It's possible to get two or three inches of rain in 15 or 20 minutes, once or twice a year. Years ago we had a succession of very hot days in late June and the first few days of July, but in spite of that I bet my brother-in-law a nickel that it would rain for the Fourth of July. The day came and the temperature was more than 100 degrees early in the day, but by midafternoon the clouds gathered and in a few minutes we had three inches of rain.

To this day I'm sorry I didn't bet much more (even though I do not remember collecting). We wondered how much more rain would have come, if we had bet a dollar. He had just moved here from the state of Washington, where it drizzles almost all the time, but he couldn't imagine the toad-stranglers we have now and then here in the New Mexico desert.

Looking out the back kitchen window, toward the Sandía Mountains, we watched the water spread across acres of land, like a flowing river. It was as much rain as I had ever seen at one time.

The damage done by that much water was incredible. We were putting an addition on the house. Unfinished adobe walls came down, and window openings allowed rooms to fill with water, destroying building materials and everything else inside. Brush, weeds and whatever the water gathered along the way plugged the culverts, causing the water to rise in the arroyos and cover the roads, causing more destruction. Crops were damaged and minds were set at ease only when the clouds dissipated and the sun shone again.

I'm glad we don't have the kind of floods they have in other parts of the country, where houses go downriver, and many square miles of homes and farms are under many feet of water. That must be dreadful!

After that rain, an incredible thing happened. The lawn filled with tiny frogs. The children were ecstatic! They ran for their little red wagon and tried to fill it up with frogs, but as fast as they put them in the wagon the frogs jumped out. The children continued their attempt to get a wagon full of frogs until darkness came, the day ended and two tired and disappointed boys went to bed. Next day there were no frogs to be found anywhere. The children's questions were not answered and neither were mine. We wondered where they came from, where they went and even whether they were frogs or toads (*sapos*).

Here we have another month of picnics, parties and birthdays for enjoyment. We work through the hot days, and the evenings are ours to celebrate. Let us not forget the Fourth of July. After all, John Adams, in 1776, believed it would be the most memorable holiday in the history of America. He hoped it would be celebrated by succeeding generations as the great anniversary festival. He wanted it celebrated with pomp and parades, with games, sports, shows, bells and bonfires from one end of the country to the other, then and forever.

The Pueblos have their special dances and hundreds of people, both tourists and natives, go there to enjoy old rituals and wonderful Native American cuisine. The squash is a native of this hemisphere, and the garden is giving generously, so let us try a recipe very desirable to both Native American and New Mexican palates.

49

Calabacitas con Carne

Squash with Meat

1 1/2 pounds beef steak, cubed

2 tablespoons shortening

1/2 cup water (approximately)

5 medium butter squash, zucchini or crookneck, diced

1 medium onion, sliced and separated into rings

2 cups whole kernel corn

1 cup chopped green chile

2 cloves garlic, minced

1 cup grated Monterey Jack cheese

❖ Brown beef in shortening in large skillet at medium-high heat. Reduce heat and add water to beef. Cover and simmer at low heat until tender. Add more water if necessary.

❖ Add remaining ingredients, except cheese, and cook at medium heat until squash is tender.

❖ Garnish with cheese before serving.

You can see that the meat is an added ingredient. Some natives prefer the squash without the meat, which is the way it is usually prepared. Any kind of squash may be used. The green and yellow squash together make for an appealing dish.

The evenings are wonderful because of the heat we have endured during the day. A drink to enjoy as we settle down is a margarita. I think of it as the favorite of most New Mexicans and it was mine for many years. Now I usually settle for much less – a root beer or a cup of coffee. But for some special occasions a special dessert is quite in order, so let us try it.

Margarita Pie

Crust:

3/4 cup pretzel chips, the lightly salted variety

1/3 cup butter, melted

3 tablespoons sugar

❖ Crush pretzel chips, combine with butter and sugar, and press into a 9-inch pie plate. Chill.

Filling:

1/2 cup fresh lemon juice

1 envelope plain gelatin

4 eggs, separated

1 cup sugar, divided in half

1/4 teaspoon salt

1 teaspoon lemon rind

1/3 cup tequila

3 tablespoons Triple Sec

❖ Mix lemon juice and gelatin and let stand until soft.

❖ Beat egg yolks and add 1/2 cup sugar, salt and lemon rind.

❖ Add gelatin and cook over boiling water, stirring constantly until it thickens.

❖ Remove from heat and blend in tequila and Triple Sec.

❖ Chill.

❖ Beat egg whites until foamy, gradually adding the remaining sugar, until stiff peaks form. Fold in cooked mixture.

❖ Spoon into crust and chill.

❖ Serves 8.

Tacos & Taco Sauce

Here's a recipe you can have some fun with. One can buy commercially prepared taco sauce, or mix together the following ingredients and refrigerate overnight.

Taco Sauce
1/2 cup olive oil

3 tablespoons lime juice

2 cloves garlic, minced

1/2 teaspoon ground black pepper

1 tablespoon ground red chile

1/2 teaspoon salt

Tacos
2 pounds ground beef

2 onions, sliced

1 clove garlic, minced

❖ Fry these three ingredients in olive oil and set aside.

12 corn tortillas

❖ Fry very briefly in oil and place on paper towel, blotting to absorb excess oil.

1 pound grated Monterey Jack cheese

2 tomatoes, cut in small cubes

1/2 head lettuce, chopped

1 onion, cut up

I like to place prepared meat, cheese, tomatoes, onions and lettuce ready to stuff, each in separate bowls and let each person make his or her own. Children love the whole process. They can gild the lily by pouring guacamole sauce or sour cream over the top of the taco.

Raspberry Delight

2 1/4 cups flour

2 tablespoons sugar

3/4 cup butter or margarine, softened

Filling:

1 package (8 ounces) cream cheese, softened

1 cup confectioners' sugar

1 teaspoon vanilla extract

1/4 teaspoon salt

2 cups whipped topping

1 package (6 ounces) raspberry gelatin

2 cups boiling water

2 packages (10 ounces each) sweetened frozen raspberries

❖ In a bowl, combine flour and sugar, blend in butter until smooth. Press into an ungreased 13-inch by 9-inch baking pan.

❖ Bake at 300 degrees for 20 to 25 minutes until set (crust will not brown).

❖ Cool.

❖ In a mixing bowl, beat cream cheese, confectioners' sugar, vanilla and salt until smooth. Fold in whipped topping and spread over crust.

❖ For topping: Dissolve gelatin in boiling water, stir in raspberries.

❖ Chill for 20 minutes.

❖ Spoon over filling.

❖ Refrigerate until set.

❖ Cut into squares and serve.

Peach Cream Pie

1 1/2 cups flour
1/2 teaspoon salt
1/2 cup butter

Filling:
4 cups fresh peaches, sliced
1 cup sugar, divided
2 tablespoons flour
1 egg
1/2 teaspoon vanilla
1/2 teaspoon salt
1 cup (8 ounces) sour cream

Topping:
1/3 cup sugar
1/3 cup flour
Pinch of cinnamon
1/4 cup butter

❖ Combine flour and salt, cut in butter until crumbly. Press into 9-inch pie plate.

❖ Place peaches in bowl, sprinkle 1/2 cup sugar.

❖ Combine flour, egg, vanilla, salt and remaining sugar; fold in sour cream.

❖ Stir into peaches; pour into crust.

❖ Bake at 400 degrees for 15 minutes. Reduce heat to 350 degrees; bake for 20 minutes.

❖ For topping: Combine sugar, flour and cinnamon in a small bowl; cut in butter until crumbly. Sprinkle over the pie.

❖ Return oven temperature to 400 degrees, and bake 15 minutes longer.

❖ Cool.

Quesitas

Note: Here is something to dip, for summer fun.

1 8-ounce package cream cheese
12 ounces grated cheddar cheese
2 4-ounce cans green chile, chopped
1 cup pecan meal (or ground pecans)

❖ Combine grated cheddar cheese and softened cream cheese, mixing well.
❖ Stir in green chiles and mix thoroughly.
❖ Form into bite-sized balls and roll in ground pecans.
❖ Chill until firm.
❖ Serve with tortilla chips and salsa picante.

PUEBLO ROOTS HELP DEFINE OUR CUISINE

The other day as I was visiting with a friend, I referred to the food we were eating as "Mexican" food. She objected and said, "It is not Mexican, it is Spanish." I backed off and said it was really New Mexican, for nowhere else could one find the wonderful chile that we were eating.

I have always thought of New Mexican food as a combination of all the ingredients different people have brought here with them. It is still changing, because people still are coming. Nevertheless, the conversation led me to come home and research how Mexican-American food in the Southwest came to be.

We know that the Spanish and Mexicans lived in the Southwest before the United States declared its independence from the British. But some forget that the Pueblo Indian was here before that. Their cuisine was based on chile, corn, beans and squash. For some reason, corn has never become part of the cuisine in Spain. A friend of ours visiting here from Spain could not understand how we could eat and enjoy corn on the cob. He was not interested in corn tortillas, tamales, enchiladas or anything made of corn. He called corn *comida de caballo*, food for horses. Besides that, each time we had chile, he exclaimed, *otro chiliazo*, meaning another mess of chile. He never tried either food and that was his loss.

Our cuisine has not always been as popular as it is now. In Texas, Arizona and California, it was hardly known until the last 30 or 40 years, in spite of the fact that all three states had Hispanic settlements. Why was this? Well, maybe because New Mexico was settled so many years before the other three states, California being the last. Our state had 223 years without outside influence, allowing the establishment of a unique indigenous culture, based on the chile, corn, beans and squash that grew well in this climate. Mexicans, Pueblo Indians and the Spanish intermarried and the cultures mixed. When trade restrictions imposed by the Spanish were eliminated after Mexican independence, outsiders began to come and influence the area.

The New Mexico-style Mexican-American cooking today contains dishes seldom, if ever, found in other parts of the Southwest. Each state has its own version of how it should be, but it doesn't compare with what we have here.

In Texas they have what they call Tex-Mex cooking, based upon the ranch country resources of beef and game with the ancho and jalapeño chiles. The chiles are used more as a spice than a vegetable. Their *chile con carne* is famous. The phrase means chile with meat, but it is really meat seasoned with chile.

In Arizona the Mexican-American food is patterned after the cuisine of the state of Sonora, which they border. They specialize in the paper-thin flour tortillas, burritos, chimichangas and *carne seca* – dried meat, or jerky. Their desert is an excellent place to make it.

In California they have retained more of the Spanish characteristics rather than the Mexican-American. Their foods have distinctive qualities because of the olives, nuts and fruits that thrive in that Mediterranean-like climate that is very similar to southern Spain's.

During the '40s I lived and worked in California. What I remember of "Mexican" foods are the refried beans and cheese made into tacos, but there was no chile of any kind. We New Mexicans went to California to work in defense plants and they saw us as coming from another planet. I was often asked if we had the same currency as they did.

I learned to love oranges that had been so rare in my childhood, but I was puzzled that you had to pay for them no matter how abundant the crop had been that year. I remembered how at home, when we had more apples than we could use, we gave them away. They were well into the money economy, and we were still depending mostly on the barter system.

In California I learned to eat avocados and loved the tightly rolled tacos swirled in avocado sauce. I lived with a passel of cousins who had been born there and they teased me terribly about New Mexico and my countrified ways. In spite of our differences, I loved them dearly and learned much from them.

Let's try a recipe of *pan dulce*, variations of which are found in Mexican-American communities from California to Texas.

Pan Dulce
Sweet Bread

2/3 cup milk

2 tablespoons shortening

2 tablespoons butter

2 eggs, beaten

1/3 cup milk

1 package dry yeast

1/2 teaspoon sugar

4 1/2 cups flour

1/2 cup sugar

2 tablespoons brown sugar

1/2 teaspoon cinnamon

1/2 tablespoon salt

❖ Heat the 2/3 cup milk just enough to melt the shortening and butter. Allow the mixture to cool to room temperature. Add the beaten eggs.

❖ Heat the 1/3 cup milk until it is room temperature and stir in the yeast and 1/2 teaspoon sugar. Allow the mixture to sit until bubbles form on the surface, then stir it into the milk and egg mixture.

❖ Mix together the flour, 1/2 cup sugar, 2 tablespoons brown sugar, the cinnamon and the salt.

❖ Stir in the yeast and milk and egg mixture to make a medium dough. Add flour or water as needed.

❖ Knead the dough or process it in a food processor. Lightly grease the dough, place it in a dish, cover it with a damp cloth and allow it to rise until doubled in size.

❖ While the dough is rising, cream together the topping ingredients.

Topping:
3/4 cup flour

3 tablespoons sugar

3 tablespoons brown sugar

1/2 teaspoon cinnamon

1/4 cup butter

2 egg yolks

3/4 teaspoon vanilla

❖ After the dough has risen, divide it into 16 balls. Roll them into circles about 3 inches in diameter and place them on baking sheets.

❖ Brush each dough circle with a mixture of 1 egg white and 2 tablespoons water.

❖ Cover them with a thin layer of the topping. At this point you may leave the topping as is or cut designs such as parallel lines into it with a thin knife.

❖ Cover the rolls and allow them to rise until doubled in size, 30 to 40 minutes.

❖ Bake the bread in 375-degree oven until done, about 20 minutes.

❖

Frijoles
Southwest Pinto Beans

2 cups beans

2 quarts water

1 tablespoon cooking oil

6 slices bacon

❖ Sort dry beans, removing stones and broken beans. Wash in saucepan. Cook in pressure cooker 45 minutes or in crockpot overnight.

❖ When beans are soft, cut up bacon and fry crisp. Pour bacon and drippings into bean pot.

❖ Add salt if needed.

Scalloped Corn

1 package (10 ounces) frozen whole kernel corn, cooked and drained or fresh
corn from the cob, cooked and drained

2 tablespoons margarine or butter

1/4 cup onion, chopped

1/2 cup green chile, chopped

2 tablespoons flour

1/2 teaspoon salt

1 teaspoon dry red chile

3/4 cup milk

1 large egg, slightly beaten

1/3 cup cracker crumbs

1 tablespoon margarine or butter, melted

❖ Heat oven to 350 degrees.

❖ Melt 2 tablespoons margarine in 1-quart saucepan over medium heat; cook
onion and green chile until tender.

❖ Stir in flour, salt and red chile. Stir until mixture is bubbly. Remove from heat.

❖ Gradually stir in milk. Heat to boiling.

❖ Stir in corn and egg and pour into ungreased casserole dish.

❖ Mix cracker and 1 tablespoon melted margarine and sprinkle over corn mixture.

❖ Bake uncovered for 30 to 35 minutes.

❖❖❖

Sopaipillas

4 cups flour

3 teaspoons baking powder

3 tablespoons shortening

1 teaspoon salt

1 1/4 to 1 1/2 cups water

❖ Sift flour, baking powder and salt together.

❖ Cut in shortening; add water.

❖ Roll out dough about 1/4-inch thick and cut into 3-inch squares.

❖ Deep fry until golden brown.

❖ Makes about 4 dozen.

Corn Pudding

1 cup canned cream-style corn

1 cup canned whole-kernel corn

2 tablespoons green peppers, finely cut

2 tablespoons mushrooms, chopped

3 tablespoons cheddar cheese, grated

1 tablespoon flour

1 tablespoon sugar

1 teaspoon salt

1/4 teaspoon pepper

1 cup milk

1 tablespoon butter

4 eggs

❖ Beat eggs until thick. Add corn, green pepper and mushrooms.

❖ Combine flour, sugar, salt and pepper in mixing bowl.

❖ Stir milk into dry ingredients and blend in melted butter.

❖ Combine with corn mixture and beat well.

❖ Pour into greased 1 1/2 quart casserole dish.

❖ Sprinkle with cheese.

❖ Bake about 1 hour and 20 minutes at 325 degrees.

Fall

We have enjoyed the beautiful colors of the cottonwood forest, up and down the Río Grande Valley. The aspen make the mountaintops spectacular. The master artist has done a great job again. Hummingbirds are still feeding. We wonder why they don't leave, since they have so far to go before the cold arrives.

Fruits and vegetables have matured, and we have enjoyed the harvest. The trees drop their leaves, just as the leaves of life keep falling, one by one. The landscape has changed, and serious cold begins to settle down.

CHILE TIME

It's chile time in New Mexico. The wonderful aroma of chile roasting up and down the streets is enough to steer you off the road or at least make you think you died and went to heaven.

The propane chile roaster is the most wonderful invention, making life easier for the New Mexico housewife. Why it didn't merit the Nobel Prize, I'll never know. The whole family has spent many long hours over a hot wood stove roasting chile. Then we peeled it, and in time long past, we strung it up to dry on a clothesline to have green chiles in mid-winter. It if looked like rain, we brought it in, only to have to hang it up again, until it was good and dry. We stored it in tight containers. Our family did not can the chile because of fear of botulism.

One summer, we were roasting chile on the wood stove in the kitchen and the work was progressing slowly. The fire was not burning well, so my mother suggested that I get some wood chips to help it along. The men had just brought in some wood from an area in the mountains where the U.S. Forest Service was widening the road. I filled a basket with chips and started a great fire in the stove. There were three of us in the large kitchen. My mother was at the sink and I was trying to convince my young son to play either outside or in the next room, when we were deafened by a terrible blast that destroyed the chile and the stove, and left us flabbergasted. Pieces of cast iron were stuck in the ceiling, and other pieces were found 30 feet away in the living room. None of us was hurt, but the chile roasting was done for the day. We figured it must have been a blasting cap dropped by the road workers and picked up by the wood gatherers and then by me into my basket of chips.

Years later, we used the backyard charcoal broiler. Often we held a barbecue at the same time so that the children would help with the roasting. It took bags of charcoal, polluted the air badly and sometimes after the meal, the roasting went on until midnight, long after guests went home. Everyone was weary and tired, and still it had to be peeled and sacked for freezing. Many families put up more than one sack of chile, so now that they roast it for you, and so easily, it's pure pleasure.

Peeling chiles isn't hard if you place them in a small plastic trash bag immediately after roasting, or wrap them in a moist kitchen towel. The steam helps to separate the skin from the flesh. Peel them while they are still warm. Also, warm, roasted chiles can be frozen whole in freezer bags, unpeeled, until you are ready to use them. Just be sure to lay them as flat as possible in the freezer bag. These peel easily when thawed.

Chile can be used in many different ways. Whenever a recipe calls for bell peppers, I insert a few green chiles. The taste of most soups and casseroles can be enhanced with chile. It is used by some as a condiment, the way some use onions and garlic. For others it is a vegetable. I cannot remember a meal in my parents' home without chile, including breakfast.

Here are a couple of recipes that you will enjoy – use as much or as little chile, hot or mild, as you desire. The cheese in these recipes can also be of your own choice.

Green Chiles Rellenos

12 to 16 whole, long, green chiles (such as Anaheim or Big Jim varieties)
1 pound Monterey Jack cheese cut in thin strips

For the batter:
1/2 cup flour
1/2 teaspoon salt
1/2 teaspoon baking powder
1 egg
1 cup milk

❖ Roast and peel the green chile peppers, removing seeds and stems. Try to keep the chile flesh whole. Make a slit in the chile just large enough to insert strips of cheese. Some cooks prefer to leave stems on, so cut a neat slit down the side of the chile to remove seeds and to insert cheese.

❖ Mix flour, salt and baking powder.

❖ Add milk and egg and beat until smooth.

❖ Dip cheese-stuffed chiles in batter and fry in about 1 inch of hot fat (vegetable oil) until golden brown.

❖ Drain.

Ideally, these are served hot with pinto beans.

Southwest Chile Pie

1 baked 9-inch pie shell
1 1/2 cups crushed tortilla chips
2 cups leftover cooked pinto beans
2 cups green chile, diced
1/4 cup sliced green onions
1/2 cup sour cream
1/2 cup shredded Monterey Jack cheese
1/2 cup shredded cheddar cheese
2 1/2 ounce jar of sliced mushrooms
Sliced ripe olives

❖ Preheat oven to 375 degrees.

❖ Sprinkle 1 cup of chips in piecrust.

❖ Combine beans, chile and onions; spread over chips in piecrust. Dot with sour cream.

❖ Top with mushrooms and olives, then cheese, finally the rest of the chips.

❖ Cover lightly with foil and bake for about 15 minutes. Uncover and bake 30 minutes longer.

❖ Garnish with tomatoes and avocados, if desired.

❖

Red Enchiladas

12 corn tortillas (blue, if desired)

1/2 cup vegetable oil

3 cups longhorn cheese, grated

2 small onions (optional)

4 eggs

❖ Fry tortillas in oil until soft and drain on paper towels.

❖ Layer tortillas on serving plates, topping each with cheese, onions (if desired) and chile sauce.

❖ Fry tortillas in oil until soft and drain on paper towels.

❖ Layer tortillas on serving plates, topping each with cheese, onions (if desired) and chile sauce.

❖ Stack two or three per plate and top with cheese and more chile sauce.

❖ Allow cheese to melt by placing plates in warm oven, while you fry the eggs in the remaining oil.

❖ Top each enchilada with a fried egg – or maybe you prefer to top it with sour cream. Serve immediately.

❖ Serves 4.

Red Chile Sauce

2 tablespoons olive oil

2 tablespoons flour (optional)

2 pounds pork, or chicken

2 cloves garlic, or garlic salt

1/2 cup chile powder

2 cups water or broth

Salt to taste

Most recipes call for flour, but you want a rich, red, tasty chile sauce, not a gravy. My mother used flour to cut the heat, so that we children would eat it and also to increase the amount.

❖ Sauté garlic in oil.
❖ Cut pork into bite-sized pieces and cook in oil where garlic has been sautéed. Do not overcook meat.
❖ Add chile powder and water or broth. Simmer to desired consistency and season to taste.

Sweet Chiles Rellenos

There is one more chile recipe you must try, for it serves double duty as a dessert and appetizer. Perfect for festive occasions, these sweet *rellenos* (reh-yen-nos) aren't difficult to make, but require a little time and patience. Often they are served at wedding receptions or other special occasions. They are made the same as croquettes and may be prepared ahead of time and deep fried at the last minute. They also freeze well, so they can be made days ahead of the event and warmed just before serving.

2 pounds lean beef
3 cups chopped green chile
1 1/2 cups brown sugar
1 cup piñon nuts or chopped pecans
2 teaspoons allspice
3 teaspoons cinnamon
1 teaspoon salt
4 eggs
Flour

❖ Cook beef and grind fine.
❖ Mix all ingredients except flour and eggs and refrigerate overnight.
❖ Divide mixture and shape into walnut-size balls, rolling them in flour as if making croquettes. Chill at least 2 hours.
❖ Beat egg whites until stiff, then add yolks.
❖ Roll each ball in egg mixture and then fry in unsaturated oil. Handle *rellenos* carefully, so the crust is not punctured. Place on paper towel to drain.
❖ Makes about 4 dozen.

Death by Chocolate

Note: After a main dish of either red or green chile my family often craves chocolate. Here's a good recipe from my friend, Julie.

12 ounces semisweet chocolate chips

1 3/4 cups milk

2 eggs

1 devil's food cake mix

4 ounces Jell-O instant chocolate pudding

❖ Mix cake mix, milk and eggs.

❖ Add pudding and stir for two minutes.

❖ Stir in chips.

❖ Pour into greased and floured Bundt pan.

❖ Bake at 350 degrees for 55 minutes.

Best if made two days before serving.

BREAKFAST OF CHAMPIONS

As we watched "The Language of Life" with Bill Moyers on PBS, we listened to authors who were trying to understand and heal their lives through the power of poetry. Not many of us do this, though we do wonder how our lives have been shaped by what our parents did to us and what we, in turn, have done to our children. I have a true story that could make you wonder about all this.

Years ago, there was a little girl in our village whose life was being completely determined by her parents and the parents of a young man many miles away. Both sets of parents knew each other, but the young people did not. A marriage was being arranged. We think of this happening in China and other faraway places, but it also has happened here, close to home.

Letters were exchanged, discussing the young peoples' lives and the standing of the adults in their respective communities. I remember hearing that the fellow's parents were well-to-do. Those were the days when if you owned a few cattle and some other farm animals, you were rich. The correspondence went on for a long time. The mail was slow and the girl's parents were in no hurry. She was all of 15, the oldest daughter in a growing family, where there was too much work for the mother, and the daughter's absence would certainly be felt. This went on for a long time and finally the families decided to go ahead with the wedding and the date was set.

Two weeks before the wedding, mother and daughter went north to where the girl's grandmother lived, which was not far from the home of the prospective groom. The bride's whole family baked cakes, pies and *bizcochitos*. They killed a calf and other animals in preparation for the wedding.

The grandmother made the wedding dress and cake, and I can just imagine many horse and carriage trips back and forth to the only mercantile store for miles around. The family had to make do with whatever was available.

The young couple met the day before the wedding. Imagine two bashful young people seeing each other for the first time, the day before they became husband and wife. The girl was young and beautiful, and the mother-in-law immediately became her enemy. No woman could ever be worthy of her son, but she needed to test this girl nevertheless. After the wedding the couple settled down next door to the in-laws, which was common in those days. There the bride's every move could be detected and challenged, and it was.

Winter was coming and the butchering of a calf provided the test the old lady needed for proving the abilities of the young wife. The new bride was given the whole stomach of the calf and a paring knife, and sent down to the river about a mile away. She was admonished not to come back until she had cleaned it all perfectly.

The stomach, which is called honeycomb and tripe in grocery stores, we call *librillo*, which comes from the word for book. This is because a large portion of it is made up of folds which resemble the pages of a book, very difficult to clean, just as a book is sometimes difficult to understand.

It's called honeycomb because of the tiny compartments that make up the stomach wall. There are hundreds of them, and each one must be scraped to remove the inner lining. Every fold, like a page of a little book, must be scraped clean. If any of the inner lining is left, there will be an unpleasant taste in the resulting dish.

Most of my readers have no idea how difficult the job would be with hot water, let alone freezing cold river water. Imagine trying to pluck the feathers off a chicken with cold water! Same difference! But most people have never done either thing.

The poor girl worked for hours, while the old woman laughed and told neighbors how the job could never be done. The superstition was that since the girl could not do the job, she and the mother-in-law (*suegra*) would never get along.

To the old lady's disbelief, the stomach was scraped clean. The innocent girl presented it to her mother-in-law, receiving no praise, thanks or comment of any kind. That young lady was and is my oldest sister, now in her 80s. She told me it must have been a miracle, for how else could such a job be done? I have always thought she was a remarkably patient woman.

My oldest brother came up with the idea that I should offer the recipe for *menudo*, which he makes often and shares with some of the family, some of whom have trouble admitting they even like it. He calls it breakfast of champions! I, for one, like it very much. I shall cut his recipe in half, to make it more manageable. And now you see why someone must clean the cow's stomach!

Menudo

3 1/2 pounds of tripe, *librillo* (available at meat counters, already cleaned)

1 pound stewing beef, cut in small pieces (for flavoring)

2 or 3 pigs' feet

1 large onion

3 cloves garlic

3 tablespoons red chile powder or 1 cup red chile sauce

1 bag frozen hominy

Some of these ingredients are cooked separately and finally combined to make what we call *menudo*.

❖ Follow directions on package for cooking the hominy and set aside.

❖ Cook stewing meat and pigs' feet together in pressure cooker for about an hour.

❖ Cook the *librillo* in a separate pan for about 30 minutes or less so it does not dissolve.

❖ Then place all these ingredients in a large container, together with garlic, onion and red chile powder or red chile sauce for flavor and coloring.

❖ Garnish with oregano, lemon, coriander leaves (cilantro) and green onions.

Green Chile Casserole

4 cups boiled chicken, cut up

2 cans green chile, chopped

1 onion, chopped

2 cans cream of chicken soup

1 can milk, or water

1 dozen corn tortillas

2 cups cheese (cheddar is best), grated

❖ Sauté chopped onions and add chicken, chile, soup and milk.

❖ Fry tortillas in oil until soft (a very short time).

❖ Place chicken mixture in bottom of 9-inch by 12-inch pan. Cover with 3 or 4 tortillas. Cover with cheese and cover with chicken mixture.

❖ Repeat layers until mixture is used up. Last layer should be cheese.

❖ Bake at 350 degrees for 30 minutes.

Chile Pork Roast

2 teaspoons garlic salt

1 teaspoon pepper

2 teaspoons ground red chile

1 boneless rolled pork loin roast (4 to 4 1/2 pounds)

1 or 2 medium onions, sliced

1 cup water

❖ Combine garlic salt, pepper and red chile powder; rub over entire roast.

❖ Place roast with fat side up on greased rack in a roasting pan. Top with onion.

❖ Pour water into pan. Bake, uncovered, at 325 degrees for 2 to 2 1/2 hours. Let stand for 10 to 15 minutes before slicing.

❖ Yields 8 to 10 servings.

Applesauce Currant Cake

3 cups sugar (1 1/2 cups brown, 1 1/2 cups white)

1/2 cup margarine

2 eggs

1/2 teaspoon salt

2 cups flour

2 teaspoons baking soda

1 teaspoon vanilla

2 cups unsweetened applesauce

1 1/2 cups currants

1 teaspoon cinnamon

1 teaspoon allspice

- Mix first four ingredients together.
- Add flour.
- Mix applesauce and baking soda and add to previous mixture.
- Add remaining ingredients and mix.
- Bake in a 9-inch by 12-inch pan for 35 minutes at 350 degrees.

Topping:

- Melt 1/2 stick margarine.
- Add 1 cup brown sugar, 4 tablespoons milk and a dash of salt.
- Bring to a boil.
- Remove from heat and add 1 teaspoon vanilla and 1/2 cup chopped nuts.
- Pour over cake and place under broiler for one minute. Enjoy!

Wiggly Pumpkins

2 packages (6 ounces each) orange gelatin

2 1/2 cups boiling water

1 cup cold milk

1 package (3 or 4 ounces) instant vanilla pudding mix

Candy corn

Black licorice and/or gumdrops

* Dissolve gelatin in water and set aside for 30 minutes.
* Whisk milk and pudding mix until smooth, about one minute.
* Quickly pour into gelatin; mix until well blended.
* Pour into oiled 13-inch by 9-inch by 2-inch pan.
* Chill until set.
* Cut circles with biscuit cutter or pumpkin-shaped cookie cutter.
* Just before serving, add candy eyes and mouth.

These wiggly pumpkins form real festive finger snacks.

Festive Sausage Cups

Pastry for double-crust pie, 9-inch

1 pound pork sausage

6 green onions, chopped

1 tablespoon butter or margarine

1/2 cup canned mushrooms, chopped

1/4 cup stuffed olives, thinly sliced

3/4 teaspoon salt

1/4 teaspoon pepper

1/4 cup flour

2 cups whipping cream

1 cup (4 ounces) Swiss cheese, shredded

❖ On a lightly floured surface, roll pastry to 1/8-inch thickness. Cut with a 2 1/2-inch round cookie cutter.

❖ Press into the bottom and up the sides of greased miniature muffin cups.

❖ Bake at 400 degrees for 6 to 8 minutes or until lightly browned. Remove from pans to cool.

❖ In a skillet, brown sausage, drain well and set aside.

❖ In same skillet, sauté onions in butter until tender.

❖ Add mushrooms, sliced olives, salt and pepper.

❖ Sprinkle with flour. Add cream and bring to a boil, stirring constantly. Stir in sausage.

❖ Reduce heat and simmer until thickened, about 5 to 10 minutes.

❖ Spoon into pastry cups and sprinkle with cheese.

❖ Place on ungreased baking sheet and bake at 350 degrees for 10 minutes.

❖ Garnish with chopped olives.

THE LUCK OF THE DRAW

E very year in the fall, as the weather cools and hunting season comes around, I remember this old tale:

The weekend had gone as always for Ramon. He went down to the *cantina* to drink beer and listen to his friends tell the same jokes and stories he had heard all his life. He was a quiet, simple man, who listened but never said much. The evening lengthened into night and the bartender wanted to lock up and go home. Poor Ramon was too drunk to mount his horse, but someone helped him into the saddle with difficulty, then slapped the horse on the rump and sent him on his way.

The horse knew the road for he had taken this same route many times before with his unconscious rider. Once home, Ramon's widowed sister ran out and helped him off the horse, into the house and onto the cot where he slept. The horse remained saddled, standing outside until next day, when Ramon was sober enough to unsaddle him, and water and feed him.

Lying on a cot by the fireplace and listening to the crackle of cedarwood, he wondered how he got home the night before. He remembered having bought a raffle ticket with his last dollar, but couldn't be sure what they were offering as a prize. "I could have bought myself another drink or brought home a sample bottle for my cure this morning," he said to himself. The first drink of water in the morning was always the worst. He wondered what rotten food he had eaten. Better to blame the last bite than the last drink.

Just then his mother came into the room, angry as usual, because of his drinking. He didn't offer any excuses or even listen to the sermon, for it was the one he had heard the last time and the time before that.

He tried to recall the happenings of the night before and what the raffle was all about. Could it have been that beautiful rifle they had on the counter? No, they wouldn't raffle something that useful. "Wouldn't it be great if I had a new rifle!" he thought. "I'd go hunting and get us a small deer for Thanksgiving dinner. Then both my sister and mother would be happy with me."

The day was cloudy and dark. Maybe it would snow. He took care of the horse, fed the chickens and hogs and was glad to get back inside the house. He built a big fire in the fireplace and since the women were not speaking to him, he went back to his cot and slept for hours.

He thought he was dreaming, but as he listened closely, he realized someone was knocking loudly at the door. He lived several miles from the nearest town and seldom did anyone come around, least of all on Sunday. He opened the door and was surprised to find the owner of the bar standing there.

His first thought was to wonder what he had done wrong the night before to occasion this visit. In his stupor he could have done most anything. Then he noticed that the man had a rifle in his hands. He was struck with fear. But the man smiled and said, "You won the raffle!"

Ramon was totally speechless. When the truth hit him, all he could say was, "*¡Cuando a uno le toca, hasta por la chimenea entra!*" meaning that when Lady Luck smiles on you, even if you are drunk as the dickens, good luck comes in through the chimney.

In those days, turkey was not the traditional Thanksgiving dinner meat in this part of the country. Hunters were more likely to bring home a deer, which was more plentiful by far. Venison can be gamey and dry. To avoid this, the animal was washed thoroughly with vinegar water and left overnight. The meat was prepared very much like beef. It was often served with homemade salsas, using our native chiles, with onions and garlic and tomatoes. Nowadays, the variety of prepared salsas offered commercially is enough to overwhelm a person in both supermarkets and gourmet shops.

This is one of the best and most popular home-style salsas that I have tried, mostly because the ingredients called for are available in one's kitchen all the time. It is also used as the salsa for the famous *huevos rancheros*, or ranch-style eggs.

Salsa Ranchera

Ranch-Style Salsa

2 tablespoons olive oil
2 tablespoons jalapeño chiles, seeded and minced
1/2 cup onion, chopped
2 teaspoons vinegar
2 cups tomatoes, chopped
1/4 teaspoon ground black pepper
1/2 teaspoon salt, or to taste
Light beef broth or water

❖ Heat the olive oil over medium heat, add the chiles and onion, and cook until they begin to soften. Do not allow them to brown.
❖ Add the remaining ingredients except the water or broth and cook, stirring frequently, for 1/2 hour over very low heat.
❖ Add just enough broth or water to make the salsa a little soupy and continue cooking about 10 more minutes. The salsa should be thick enough to coat a spoon without running off. Add more liquid or cook a little longer, as necessary.
❖ Makes enough to serve 4 with chips or with a meal.

This is the salsa used in *huevos rancheros.*

Now let's try something a wee bit more colorful and festive.

Pumpkin Softies & Frosting

1 cup margarine, softened
3/4 cup firmly packed brown sugar
3/4 cup granulated sugar

1 egg

1 cup canned solid-pack pumpkin

1 teaspoon vanilla extract

1 3/4 cups all-purpose flour

1/4 teaspoon salt (optional)

1 teaspoon baking soda

1 teaspoon pumpkin pie spice or ground cinnamon

2 1/2 cups oats, quick or old-fashioned, uncooked

❖ Heat oven to 350 degrees.

❖ In a large bowl, beat margarine and sugars until creamy.

❖ Add pumpkin, egg and vanilla; beat well.

❖ Gradually add combined flour, baking soda, salt and pumpkin pie spice or cinnamon; mix well.

❖ Stir in oats.

❖ Drop by rounded tablespoonful onto cookie sheet. Bake 10 minutes or until brown; remove to wire rack. Cool completely.

Frosting:

1 3-ounce package cream cheese, softened

1 tablespoon milk

1/2 teaspoon vanilla extract

2 1/2 cups confectioners' sugar

Yellow and red food coloring

❖ For frosting: Beat cream cheese, milk and vanilla until smooth.

❖ Gradually beat in confectioners' sugar until blended. Tint with food coloring, if desired.

❖ Frost top of each cookie. Store tightly covered in refrigerator.

❖ Makes about 4 dozen cookies and can be made days before a fiesta.

Mexican Turkey Corn Chowder

3 cups leftover turkey, cut up

1/2 cup chopped onion

1 or 2 garlic cloves, minced

3 tablespoons butter or margarine

2 chicken bouillon cubes

1 cup hot water

1/2 teaspoon ground cumin

2 cups Half-and-Half cream

2 cups (8 ounces) Monterey Jack cheese, shredded

1 can (16 ounces) cream-style corn

1 cup green chile, chopped

1 medium tomato, chopped

Fresh cilantro, to taste

❖ In a heavy skillet sauté onions and garlic with butter and add turkey.

❖ Dissolve bouillon cubes in hot water.

❖ Add to pan along with cumin and bring to a boil.

❖ Reduce heat, cover and simmer for 5 minutes.

❖ Add cream, cheese, corn and chile.

❖ Cook and stir over low heat until cheese is melted.

❖ Stir in tomatoes.

❖ Garnish with cilantro and serve.

Cranberry & Raisin Pie

Flaky pastry for 2-crust pie

2 cups granulated sugar

2 tablespoons flour

1/4 teaspoon salt

2/3 cup water

3 cups fresh cranberries

1 cup seeded raisins

1 1/2 teaspoons grated lemon rind

2 tablespoons melted butter

Milk

* Line a 9-inch pie plate with pastry.
* Mix sugar, flour, salt and water together and heat until sugar is melted.
* Add washed cranberries and cook slowly until skins pop open.
* Add raisins and cook 5 minutes longer.
* Add lemon rind and butter and mix lightly with fork.
* Pour into lined pie plate and adjust top crust.
* Brush top with milk.
* Bake in hot oven at 425 degrees for 40 minutes, or until brown.

A lattice top will make it look more festive.

Piecrust

(For two-crust, 8-inch or 9-inch pie)

2 cups flour

1 teaspoon salt

2/3 cup plus 2 tablespoons shortening

5 tablespoons ice water (spooned from cup with ice cubes floating in water)

❖ Mix ingredients and sprinkle water in, a tablespoon at a time, until all flour is moistened and dough almost cleans the side of the bowl.

❖ For easy handling of dough, cut in half and place between two pieces of waxed paper. Roll flat.

You are now ready to follow any pie recipe you like.

Squash Pie

1 unbaked 9-inch pie shell

1 3/4 cup squash, cooked, strained and mashed

1 cup sugar

1 teaspoon salt

1 teaspoon cinnamon

1/2 teaspoon nutmeg

1/2 teaspoon ginger

3 eggs

1 1/2 cup milk

1 tablespoon margarine or butter, melted

❖ Combine squash, sugar, salt and spices.

❖ Blend in eggs and margarine or butter.

❖ Pour into pie shell.

❖ Bake in hot oven (400 degrees) for 50 minutes, or until butter knife inserted 1 inch from pie's edge comes out clean.

Chile Eggplant Casserole

2 tablespoons olive oil

2 eggs, beaten

1/4 cup milk

1 large, or 2 small eggplants, cut into 1/2-inch slices

1 cup bread crumbs

1 can stewed tomatoes

2 cups green chile, diced

1 onion, diced

1 pound mozzarella cheese

1/4 cup Parmesan cheese

❖ Heat oil in large skillet.

❖ Dip eggplant slices into egg/milk mixture, then into bread crumbs. Fry in hot oil until golden brown on both sides.

❖ Place half of the eggplant slices in bottom of ungreased 13-inch by 9-inch casserole.

❖ Spread half of stewed tomatoes, chile, diced onions and grated cheese over eggplant. Repeat with a second layer of eggplant; repeat other vegetables.

❖ Sprinkle Parmesan cheese on top.

❖ Cover and bake in preheated oven at 350 degrees for 45 minutes. Uncover and bake an additional 15 minutes.

Walnut Chicken

2 tablespoons minced fresh ginger

1 tablespoon cornstarch

3 tablespoons soy sauce

1 tablespoon rice wine

2 cloves garlic, minced

1/2 teaspoon red pepper flakes

1 1/2 pounds boneless skinless chicken thighs, diced

3 tablespoons olive oil

3/4 cup walnut halves or pieces

3/4 cup sliced water chestnuts

1 cup frozen cut green beans, thawed

2 green onions with tops, cut into 1/2-inch pieces

1/4 cup water

Hot cooked rice

❖ Combine ginger, cornstarch, soy sauce, wine, garlic and red pepper in large bowl; stir until smooth.

❖ Add chicken; toss. Marinate 10 minutes.

❖ Heat wok or large skillet over high heat about 1 minute or until hot. Drizzle oil into wok and heat 30 seconds.

❖ Add walnuts; stir-fry about one minute or until lightly browned. Remove to small bowl.

❖ Add chicken mixture to wok; stir-fry about 6 minutes or until chicken is no longer pink in center.

❖ Add beans, water chestnuts, onions and water; stir-fry until heated through.

❖ Serve over rice and sprinkle with walnuts.

Winter

Because the days are short, each mile feels like two in winter. Dark when we get up and dark when we eat our dinner. The evenings seem too long, and we are thankful for a fire in the fireplace.

We love the sunshine; several cloudy days in a row depress us. Snow comes to the mountains and skiers rejoice. Snow comes to the valleys and the driving gets tricky. Yet there is nothing more beautiful than a world covered with snow.

The Earth rests and so must we. Our energies are spent and it is time to catch up with our reading and correspondence, time to reach for the world out there.

TASTY TAMALES

"Tradition is something vital that unites the past to the present and generates life for the future."
—Anonymous

I remember being taken as a little girl to see the Christmas light displays in Madrid, a coal-mining town on the road between Tijeras Canyon and Cerrillos. No one had ever explained anything to me about make-believe, so I thought that all I saw was real.

How could such a wonderful world exist without my having known of it before, and why did we have to leave, when such marvelous and beautiful things were in such abundance? I went home believing that I had seen real angels and Joseph and Mary, and that all the fairy-tale characters I had ever heard about were real.

During the 1930s, Madrid had one of the grandest outside productions of the Christmas story ever seen. The superintendent of mines was a man named Oscar Huber. He and the residents came up with the idea of putting a gigantic Christmas production in a natural setting. The surrounding valley and hills were the stage, and all the residents played important roles in making costumes and life-size displays.

After working all day in the mine, the men made and painted displays, built roads, strung electric wires up the mountainsides and installed transmitters for the public address system, for music and for 50,000 lights. Some displays were 75-feet long and 18- to 35-feet high. The giant Christmas tree was made up of 25 large evergreen trees wired to a pole 90 feet tall that stood 400 feet above the valley floor. A 14-foot star shone over everything. A small mining town of 1,500 persons welcomed more than 100,000 visitors from all over the world.

The angel, or trumpeter, outlined in lights, came down from atop the mountain to settle over the life-sized manger with a complete Nativity scene. At the same time, a voice proclaimed the tidings of great joy, followed by wonderful music.

Over on the baseball field they created a children's heaven, a fairyland for sure. There was a small train that went around the town full of wonders, piloted by Santa himself, who gave rides and goodies to the children. From there we made our way back home, to make our tamales, *bizcochitos* and other special foods for the holidays.

Tamales

4 pounds pork shoulder

6 cups water

6 to 8 tablespoons chile powder

1/8 teaspoon oregano (if desired)

1/4 teaspoon cumin (if desired)

2 cloves garlic, chopped fine

Salt, to taste

❖ Boil meat in water until tender. Remove meat from broth, saving broth for making dough and chile.

❖ Chop meat in 1/4-inch pieces and place in pan.

❖ Dissolve chile powder in 1 1/2 cups of the meat broth, add to the meat.

❖ Add garlic, spices and salt, and cook until almost dry.

Set aside, while preparing dough (*masa*).

Masa for Tamales

5-pound bag of prepared cornmeal *masa* flour
1 pound lard
Pork broth (from above)

❖ Cream the lard in a medium-sized mixing bowl, using a mixer at medium speed.
❖ Add flour and mix.
❖ Add enough of the broth to make the dough spreadable with a table knife.

Assembling the Tamales

❖ Rinse cornhusks and soak in warm water until pliable.
❖ Spread the center portion of each husk with 2 tablespoons of the *masa* mixture.
❖ Top with the chile-meat filling. Varied amounts of either the *masa* or the filling may be used (some like them thin, some like more of the filling).
❖ Fold the sides of the husk toward the center, the bottom of the husk up and the top down.
❖ Tie each tamale with a narrow cornhusk strip.
❖ Pour 2 inches of water into a large kettle and arrange the tamales on a rack above water level. Steam tamales for about 40 minutes.

This assembly process is more fun if it is a family or group production. After the ingredients are ready, gather the group and have some prepare the husks and cut ties; others can spread the *masa* on the husks, others can spread the filling, and others can do the tying and stacking of tamales in the steamer.

Bizcochitos

2 cups shortening

1 1/4 cup sugar

3 egg yolks or 2 whole eggs

2 tablespoons vanilla

2 teaspoons anise seed

6 cups sifted flour

3 teaspoons baking powder

1/4 cup water

1 teaspoon salt

7 tablespoons wine

❖ Cream sugar and shortening until light and fluffy.

❖ Add anise seed and beaten egg yolks, beating for a few seconds.

❖ Sift flour, baking powder and salt together. Add to first mixture.

❖ Add water and mix well.

❖ Roll out and cut with fancy cookie cutter.

❖ Sprinkle with a mixture of sugar and cinnamon.

❖ Bake at 400 degrees for 12 minutes, or until golden brown.

❖ Makes about 10 dozen small cookies.

❖

Christmas Cake

1 cup butter (or margarine)

2 cups sugar

4 eggs

4 cups sifted flour

1 teaspoon soda

1/2 teaspoon salt

1 1/2 cups buttermilk

1 tablespoon grated orange rind

1 cup chopped nuts (pecans or walnuts)

1 8-ounce package dates, chopped

❖ Cream together sugar and butter.

❖ Beat eggs and add to butter and sugar.

❖ Sift together flour, soda and salt, and add to creamed mixture, alternating with buttermilk.

❖ Add orange rind, dates and pecans.

❖ Pour into greased and floured tube pan.

❖ Bake at 325 degrees for 1 1/2 hours.

❖ While still hot, before removing from pan, punch a lot of holes in cake all the way to the bottom of the pan with an ice pick.

❖

Glaze for Christmas Cake

1 cup orange juice

2 cups sugar

2 tablespoons grated orange rind

❖ Dissolve sugar and orange juice in small saucepan over medium heat. Do not boil. Add rind.

❖ Pour hot glaze over cake. Let glaze drip into holes in cake. If cake has not pulled away from sides of tube or pan, loosen with a knife, so that some of the glaze runs down the sides and center of the cake.

❖ Let cake stand in pan for several hours. Cake must be entirely cool before removing from pan.

❖ Decorate top of cake with pecans, or cover top with a paper doily and sprinkle powdered sugar, making a festive design.

❖ This cake freezes well.

Empanaditas

Filling:

2 pounds cooked beef or 1 pound each of beef and pork

2 cups prepared minced meat

1/2 cup piñon nuts (or chopped pecans)

1/2 teaspoon allspice

1 teaspoon nutmeg

3/4 cup sugar

1 teaspoon salt

❖ Boil meat until tender. Cool and grind fine.

❖ Add minced meat, spices, nuts and sugar until filling becomes thick and moist. If filling is too dry add a little dark corn syrup.

Masa:

1/2 package yeast

3 cups lukewarm water

1 1/2 tablespoons sugar

1 1/2 teaspoons salt

1 egg

4 tablespoons shortening

6 cups flour

❖ Place yeast, sugar and salt in mixing bowl. Add water and mix until dissolved.

❖ Add beaten egg and melted shortening, adding enough flour for a dry dough.

❖ Roll out dough 1/8-inch thick, cut with round cookie cutter into discs about 4 inches in diameter.

❖ Place 1 heaping teaspoon of filling in center of patty. Fold over and pinch edges

together so that dough will seal filling.
+ Deep fry until golden brown.
+ Makes about 6 dozen.

Rice-stuffed Cornish Hens

The special rice stuffing with cinnamon, sweet raisins and honey goes well with the birds and makes a special meal for the season.

3/4 cup onions, chopped
3/4 cup celery, chopped
1/2 cup butter, divided
3 cups cooked rice
3/4 cup raisins
1/3 cup walnuts, chopped
4 tablespoons honey
2 tablespoons lemon juice
3/4 teaspoon ground cinnamon
1/2 teaspoon salt
1/8 teaspoon pepper
6 Cornish game hens (about 20 ounces each)

+ Sauté onions and celery in 3 tablespoons butter, until tender.
+ Remove from heat and add rice, raisins, walnuts, honey, lemon juice, cinnamon, salt and pepper. Mix well.
+ Stuff hens.
+ Place on rack in a large, shallow baking pan.
+ Soften the remaining butter and rub over skins.
+ Bake uncovered at 375 degrees for 1 hour, or until the juices run clear.
+ Serves 6.

BRING IN THE NEW YEAR WITH POSOLE

In the villages throughout New Mexico, New Year's Eve was a time when family and friends gathered to celebrate the passing of the old year and the welcoming of the new. The children were allowed to stay up until midnight, while adults ate and drank the hours away. In our family it was a time to review the happenings and accomplishments of the past year and make plans or resolutions for the year to come. For us children, most resolutions were broken early in the year, especially if they had to do with our conduct or grades in school, but perhaps the idea had merit in any case.

New Year's Eve was special in many ways. The young fellows in the villages hauled out a guitar or two and went from house to house singing Las Mañanitas, especially if there were young ladies in the house. There were four of us teen-age girls at home and we looked forward to all of this. Just imagine, being serenaded by young fellows! We looked forward to the guitar music and the singing, particularly because they were serenading us. This doesn't happen nowadays, as it did in the '30s and '40s. The eating and drinking still goes on, but not the singing and serenading.

My father was very strict with us, however, and since it was always midnight before the serenaders arrived at our house, he only grudgingly let them in. He fed them posole if they wanted some, and always gave them a glass of homemade wine. Then they sang again, as a way of thanking the household for the goodies, and also as a serenade to us.

"Estas son las mañanitas
que cantaba el Rey David
a las muchachas bonitas—
se las cantamos aquí.

"Despierta, mi bien, despierta,
mira que ya amaneció
ya los pajarillos cantan
la luna ya se metió."

What a lovely way to end a day after all the cooking, baking and eating with family and friends who stopped by – to have these young fellows make you feel beautiful and special with their songs. Perhaps we have become too sophisticated for all this, but the memories are fine.

Almost everyone you talk to about it has her own way of making posole. It is easy to make and feeds many. It's a generous meal. *Posole* was and still is eaten more often than once a year, but it is the traditional meal for New Year's Eve. It can be made with red or green chile, either of which can be made separately to give people a choice of which they want to put in their *posole*.

The principal ingredient in *posole* is specially treated corn, which can be obtained in three ways: homemade, canned (called hominy) or frozen (called *posole*). In my youth homemade *posole* was the only one available, and it required a lot of time to prepare. We put white corn kernels into slack lime and water. The lime came from a builders' supply or fertilizer store. We dissolved the lime in water, added the corn kernels and boiled it for about an hour. Then we had to rinse it with cold water, rubbing the kernels with our fingers until the dark corn tips were removed. Then we cooked it until the kernels burst, like popcorn. I remember taking the pan out to the water pump and nearly freezing my hands, pumping water and washing the lime off the kernels. I highly recommend using hominy or frozen *posole*.

My favorite recipe is on the following page.

Posole

(Serves 12)

1/2 package of frozen *posole* (comes in 32-ounce bag)

2 quarts water

2 1/2 to 3 pounds pork, cut in bite-sized chunks

8 to 10 roasted, peeled (seeds removed) green chiles (probably from the freezer), chopped

1 medium onion, chopped

1 clove garlic, chopped

1 or 2 16-ounce cans stewed tomatoes (depending on how hot the chile is, and how hot one likes it)

❖ Boil *posole* about 2 hours, until it pops.

❖ Add pork, onion and garlic. Boil until meat is cooked, about 1 hour, on medium heat.

❖ Add chile and tomatoes, and season with salt to taste.

The tomatoes cut the "hotness" of the chile (acid neutralizes the base), and gives a tangy flavor. Chicken also makes good *posole* and is often used in place of pork.

As a child I did not like onions. I believed that my mother used too much onion in absolutely every meal she cooked. So *posole* was not my dish, the way she made it – until one day she sent me across the village with a pitcher of *posole* for a neighbor. The day was hot, and as I wandered away, barefoot, I looked for a shady spot to wile away the time and rest. I stopped beside the Presbyterian Church, under a weeping willow tree and put my feet in the cool ditch water that was gurgling by. I carefully placed the pitcher so it wouldn't spill and removed the top to see what it looked like inside. It reminded me of popcorn. I took a kernel and ate it, and found it good. I took some more. Soon I found a piece of meat (rare in those days), and the eating became more interesting. I must have been hungry, because I ate my fill and found it very good. But I knew I had done the wrong thing. I continued to the neighbor's and when she discovered the dish, she scolded me for having stuck my fingers in the food. I handed her the pitcher and took off running, not wanting to hear her, feeling guilty and knowing the story would get back to my mother anyway. But I learned to like *posole*!

Hot Artichoke Appetizer

2 cans (10 ounces) artichoke hearts, drained and quartered
2 cups mayonnaise
2 cups Parmesan cheese, grated
Crackers

+ Drain artichoke hearts, mix mayonnaise and cheese.
+ Add all ingredients together.
+ Place in a quiche pan or shallow pan.
+ Bake at 350 degrees for 20 minutes, and serve hot on crackers.

Cranberry Pecan Pie

The following recipe is appropriate for the holidays. The cranberries offer a nice contrast to the sweetness of pecan pie and add a touch of color.

1 9-inch unbaked pastry shell
1 cup fresh cranberries, chopped
3 eggs
1 cup dark corn syrup
2/3 cup sugar
4 tablespoons butter or margarine, melted
1/2 teaspoon cinnamon
1/8 teaspoon nutmeg
1 cup pecan halves

✤ Prepare pastry shell and flute edges as desired or press with fork to decorate edges.
✤ Sprinkle cranberries into the pie shell.
✤ In bowl, beat eggs with the syrup, sugar, butter, cinnamon and nutmeg until mixture is well blended but not foamy. Pour over cranberries.
✤ Carefully arrange the pecan halves in a series of circles over the filling.
✤ Bake at 325 degrees for 50 to 55 minutes, or until a knife inserted in the center comes out clean. Be sure not to overbake the filling.

The pie might still jiggle a little when the knife comes out clean, but it will firm up. This pie is especially good served chilled with sweetened whipped cream.

No-salt Truth-serum Margaritas

2 cans (6 ounces) frozen limeade
Use same limeade can to measure the following:
2 cans water
1 can Triple Sec
2 cans Cuervo Gold tequila

❖ Mix and serve over ice cubes. Makes 10 4-ounce drinks.

Tequila Sunrise

This drink is made one drink at a time in the user's glass.

❖ Pour 1 1/2-ounces tequila over ice in a tall glass.
❖ Fill the glass with orange juice, add a dollop of grenadine, and serve with a maraschino cherry or a slice of orange

Roast Lamb Shoulder with Dressing

4 pounds lamb shoulder
2 teaspoons salt
1/4 teaspoon curry powder
1/2 teaspoon paprika
1 teaspoon salt
Pinch of dry mustard
2 tablespoons onions, chopped
1 cup celery, chopped
6 cups coarse dry bread crumbs
2 egg yolks, beaten
1 cup milk
2 tablespoons butter, melted

❖ Wipe meat thoroughly with a damp cloth. If butcher has not made pocket, split open and remove bones, cutting so meat can be rolled around the dressing. (Simmer the bones for soup or gravy.)

❖ Rub meat inside and out with the 2 teaspoons salt.

❖ Combine the next 6 ingredients, and mix thoroughly with the dry crumbs.

❖ Beat egg yolks, add the milk and melted butter, and mix with the seasoned crumbs. Let stand until all the liquid has been soaked up.

❖ Pack dressing lightly into pocket of meat and fasten with skewers and string.

❖ Place in open roasting pan and bake in a slow oven (300 degrees), allowing 35 minutes for each pound of meat.

❖ Make gravy using broth from bones.

❖ Yield: 8 to 10 servings.

Raisin Delicious

1/2 cup brown sugar, packed

1/2 cup white sugar

1 1/2 cups boiling water

1 tablespoon butter

1/4 teaspoon salt

1/4 teaspoon cinnamon

3/4 cup raisins

1 teaspoon vanilla

2 tablespoons butter

1/3 cup white sugar

3/4 cup all-purpose flour

1 teaspoon baking powder

1/4 teaspoon salt

1/3 cup milk

1/3 cup nuts, coarsely chopped

❖ Mix first 7 ingredients in saucepan and boil to a medium syrup, about 15 minutes. Remove from heat and add vanilla.

❖ Meanwhile, prepare drop batter as follows: Cream butter, add sugar and cream until blended. Sift flour, measure and resift with baking powder and salt. Add to sugar-butter mixture and combine well. Add milk all at once and stir until dry ingredients are thoroughly blended.

❖ Drop batter from tablespoon into a well-buttered baking pan (9 inches by 9 inches) and pour the raisin syrup over it.

❖ Sprinkle with nuts and bake in a moderate oven (350 degrees) for about 30 minutes or until golden brown.

❖ Serve warm or cold with cream.

SURVIVE THE DICEY WEATHER WITH SPICY COMIDA

If we have survived the holidays we can make it through the month of February. It has sunny days with little heat, cold wind, rain, snow and who knows what else. No wonder we natives call it *febrero loco*. When someone is born in February, we say she's going to be changeable, like the month of February, a little *loca*. It's as silly and as much fun as saying, "She's a Pisces."

A university student introduced me to her pre-school daughter. I asked the child, "Oh, are you a Martinez?"

She replied, "No, I'm a Sagittarius."

On another occasion, a traveler asked the waitress in a café in Socorro whether she was a Taurus. She said, "No, I'm a Chavez." She thought she was asking if she was a Torres.

Febrero loco. February is undependable in its ever-changing personality, but we know nothing lasts forever, and so we wait for the weather to change.

Persons coming to New Mexico for the first time often say that this is a harsh land. They're not used to seeing bare dirt. They observe a country destitute of vegetation, and it appears to be a barren and cheerless land. Tumbleweeds roll across what they see as empty space, and they wonder how we can live here.

These newcomers have come away from profuse greenery. They have also left behind a feeling of crowded congestion, and some of them catch on to what we have here. They call it "the wide open spaces." They leave the rush and tension of the teeming cities and find sanctuary here.

Variety is what this land offers. We have mountain ranges with towering peaks. We have deep, awe-inspiring canyons. We have the only river-bottom cottonwood forest in the world. We have seemingly endless flat mesas, which permit gorgeous panoramic views that take the eye and the mind toward the beyond.

The sky is high and wide and the sun is brilliant. Artists come because "there's something about the light." Writers and mystics come, agreeing with our state slogan, and going deeper –"The Land of Enchantment." A concept from Zen philosophy comes to mind easily in New Mexico: "the meaningfulness of empty space."

Ancient astronomers studied empty space from here. The ruins at Bandelier, Chaco Canyon and Mesa Verde in Colorado served as triangulation points for scholars who understood the sky better than most of us.

Charles F. Lummis wrote in *The Land of Poco Tiempo*, in 1928: "Sun, silence, and adobe – that is New Mexico in three words." I remember as a little girl, standing beside an adobe wall, barefoot, absorbing those three things. A small airplane whirring high above was the only noise. I didn't realize the airplane, which was a novelty then, would eventually make the silence disappear.

New Mexico includes a wide range of phenomena, from prehistoric ruins to the most modern nuclear testing laboratories. People have come from all over to live and work here. We hear ancient native languages, Spanish, English and a variety of modern Asian tongues. These languages add to the richness of our state and are in no way a danger.

Many old adobe houses still have their *hornos* (ovens) in the backyard, and even outdoor plumbing, while a TV antenna crowns the roof and a pick-up truck is parked where the hitching post used to be. We are able to combine the best of the old and the new in a happy compromise.

Our towns have both Oriental and Mexican fast food, but factory-cooked pinto beans, tacos, tamales, chile, fried rice or chop suey will never replace the homemade kind.

Black Bean Soup

1 cup black beans

1 tablespoon olive oil

1 clove garlic, minced

1/4 cup celery, diced

1/2 cup carrots, diced

1 cup onions, minced

8 cups chicken broth

1/2 teaspoon salt

Garnish:

2 hard boiled eggs, chopped

Green onion, chopped

1 cup chopped green chile

❖ Soak the beans and place washed beans in bowl, covered with cold water. Let stand overnight or at least 8 hours. If you do not soak them, place washed beans in a pot with 4 cups of water and bring to a boil. Cook for 2 minutes, turn off heat and let stand for 1 hour.

❖ Drain the soaked beans, add the broth and bring to a boil. Reduce the heat to a simmer and partially cover the pan. Cook for 2 or 3 hours or until the beans are thoroughly cooked.

❖ In a heavy skillet, heat olive oil, add onion and garlic, and cook them over low heat until the onions are transparent. Add the celery and carrots and cook the mixture, stirring for a few minutes longer.

❖ Add the vegetables to the beans, salt to taste and simmer the soup for another 30 minutes.

❖ Puree the soup in a blender or food processor. Serve the soup hot with the garnish you desire.

Frontier Soup

1 turkey or chicken breast

2 cans (14 1/2 ounces each) chicken broth, or 1 can broth and 1 can water

1 celery top

1 medium onion, sliced

1 bay leaf

1 can (15 1/2 ounces) garbanzo beans

1/2 cup canned or frozen green chile, chopped

1 teaspoon dried oregano leaves

1 cup Monterey Jack cheese, diced

Freshly cracked black pepper

❖ Simmer turkey or chicken with the broth, celery, onion and bay leaf for 35 minutes covered with lid, until vegetables are tender.

❖ Strain the broth and dice the meat.

❖ Stir in the garbanzo beans and bean liquid, chile and oregano.

❖ Return meat to pot. Simmer uncovered for 5 minutes.

❖ Serve in large soup bowls. Top with cheese cubes, if desired, and sprinkle with black pepper.

❖ The green chile adds to the Western flavor.

❖ Serve with chile cornbread.

❖ This recipe serves 4 and can be doubled.

This recipe comes from *Savoring The Southwest*, a cookbook by the Roswell Symphony Guild, with a few variations. It is very good and a cup of unsweetened applesauce may be substituted for the pumpkin to make an apple torte.

Pumpkin Torte

Crust:
2 cups crushed graham crackers

1/2 cup butter

Cream Cheese Mixture:
2 eggs, beaten

1/2 cup sugar

8 ounces cream cheese, softened to room temperature

Pumpkin Mixture:
1 cup pumpkin

3 eggs, separated

1/2 cup sugar

1 cup milk

1/2 teaspoon salt

1 1/2 teaspoons cinnamon

1 teaspoon nutmeg

1/2 teaspoon ginger

1 envelope plain gelatin

2 tablespoons butter

1/4 cup cold water

1 cup heavy cream, whipped

❖ Mix crushed graham crackers and butter and press into 9-inch by 13-inch pan.

❖ Mix the two beaten eggs, sugar and cream cheese and pour over crust.

❖ Bake for 20 minutes at 350 degrees.

❖ Beat egg yolks and mix with pumpkin, sugar, milk, salt and spices. Cook until thickened.

❖ Remove from heat.

❖ Add one envelope of plain gelatin dissolved in 1/4-cup cold water. Cool.

❖ Beat 3 egg whites to soft peaks.

❖ Add 1/2 cup sugar gradually and beat until stiff. Fold into pumpkin mixture.

❖ Pour over crust and chill. Served topped with whipped cream.

❖ Serves 10 to 12.

Mexican-style Chicken

4 split chicken breasts

1 package (8 ounces) of your favorite dry stuffing

2 green chiles, roasted and peeled

2 red chiles, roasted and peeled

1 can cream of mushroom soup

1 pint sour cream

1 1/2 cups broth

1 stick margarine, melted

1/4 pound Monterey Jack cheese

Onions

✤ Boil chicken with onions and reserve 1 1/2 cups of the broth.

✤ Set aside 1/2-cup stuffing. Place remainder of stuffing in 9-inch by 12-inch pan. Place chicken on top.

✤ Combine sour cream and soup and pour over chicken. Sprinkle with the remaining stuffing.

✤ Split both green and red chiles in half lengthwise and remove seeds. Cut in long strips and place over chicken in a decorative manner.

✤ Combine broth and margarine and pour over all ingredients.

✤ Bake for 35 minutes at 350 degrees.

✤ Place slices of cheese over chile and bake for another 5 minutes or until cheese is melted. This recipe is also good with slices of leftover turkey breast.

✤ Serves 6 to 8.

Green Chile Omelet

Omelets were a great way to incorporate whatever vegetables were available, plus eggs, which were plentiful. When I first heard the word tortilla in Spain, I mistook it for what I was hungry for, one of our tortillas. Wrong! It translated to omelet. Here we call an omelet *torta de huevo*. Let's try a zesty one with green chile and onions.

2 tablespoons olive oil
1 cup *chorizo* or ground beef
4 medium potatoes, diced and boiled for 5 minutes or until soft
1 medium onion, chopped
1 cup long green chiles, chopped (roasted and peeled, or canned)
8 eggs, mixed together as for scrambled eggs
Salt and pepper to taste
2 1/2 tablespoons olive oil
1 1/2 cups grated cheese of your choice
1 tablespoon parsley, minced

❖ Brown the *chorizo* or beef in olive oil over medium heat. Add the onion, potatoes and green chile and continue cooking until the vegetables are soft.

❖ Remove the vegetable mixture to a bowl and add the eggs, salt and pepper.

❖ Preheat oven broiler.

❖ Place large skillet over medium heat and add remaining 2 1/2 tablespoons olive oil. When the oil is hot, add the egg and vegetable mixture, making sure it covers the bottom of the pan evenly.

❖ Turn the heat to medium low and continue to cook without touching the eggs until they are well set.

❖ When they are cooked on the bottom but not completely cooked on top, finish them by placing the skillet under the broiler until the top is just beginning to brown.

❖ To serve, loosen the tortilla from the pan with a spatula and invert the skillet over a serving platter. This must be done quickly and firmly to keep the tortilla flat.

❖ Top with the cheese and parsley, if desired.

Honey Bran Muffins

1/2 cup oatmeal

1 cup oat bran

1/2 cup flour

2 teaspoons baking powder

1/2 teaspoon salt

1/2 teaspoon cinnamon

3 egg whites

1 cup honey

2 tablespoons oil

1 1/2 cups plain yogurt

❖ Preheat oven to 400 degrees.

❖ Lightly coat muffin tin with oil or place paper liners in tins.

❖ In a mixing bowl, combine oatmeal, oat bran, flour, baking powder, salt and cinnamon.

❖ In another bowl, mix egg whites, honey, oil and yogurt until well blended.

❖ Stir liquids into flour mixture just until blended.

❖ Pour batter into muffin tins to fill each 2/3 full.

❖ Bake for 20 minutes.

❖ Yields 20 large muffins.

Garlic Soup

Sopa de Ajo

6 slices of bread (may be stale)

2 tablespoons olive oil

2 cloves garlic

1 teaspoon paprika

4 eggs

Salt to taste

3 glasses water

❖ Toast bread, cut into cubes and place in a baking dish.

❖ Mince garlic and sauté in olive oil. Add paprika and pour into baking dish.

❖ Season and add water. Cook on medium heat for 1/2 hour.

❖ Just before serving poach the eggs in the soup.

❖ Serves 4.

According to the recipe book we bought in Spain, *"Esta sopa es muy apetitosa y sana."* (This soup is very tasty and good for you.)

Honey-apple Pork Chops

4 boneless pork chops, about 1-inch thick

1 1/2 cups apple cider

1/4 cup lemon juice

1/4 cup soy sauce

3 tablespoons honey

1 clove garlic, minced

1/4 teaspoon pepper

❖ Combine all ingredients, except pork chops, and mix well.

❖ Place chops in shallow dish, pour marinade over chops. Cover and refrigerate overnight, turning meat occasionally.

❖ Remove pork chops from marinade.

❖ Grill for 10 to 15 minutes, turning once and basting with marinade.

Glossary

Burrito: A flour tortilla wrapped around a filling of beans and sauce.

Chicos: Dried sweet corn kernels.

Chile pequins: Crushed dried chile seeds.

Enchilada: A cornmeal tortilla wrapped around or layered with meat, chicken or cheese and covered with red or green chile sauce.

Flan: Baked custard; crème caramel.

Frijoles: Beans (usually pinto beans).

Frijoles refritos: Refried beans.

Horno: A beehive-shaped outdoor oven of Spanish-Moorish origin, used by Spanish-speaking and Pueblo Indian cooks.

Huevos: Eggs.

Masa harina: Specially ground cornmeal for making tortillas and tamales.

Natillas: Boiled egg custard pudding.

Piñon nuts: The nuts from the pinecones of the piñon tree.

Posole: Corn kernels that have been treated with lime; hominy.

Ristra: A string of chiles tied together to hang up to dry.

Taco: A sandwich made of a cornmeal tortilla folded around meat, beans or cheese.

Tamál, tamale: Thick *masa harina* wrapped around a spicy meat filling, enclosed in cornhusks and steamed.

Tortilla: A thin, flat cake made of special blue or yellow cornmeal (*masa harina*) or flour. The tortilla is the basis of many New Mexican recipes.

Tostado: A toasted or fried piece of cornmeal tortilla.

Index